Interpreters
and the Legal Process

Joan Colin is a justice of the peace and an independent trainer of interpreters and lawyers in relation to topics covered in this book. She is a member of the Institute of Personnel and Development and a one-time Training Officer at the Magistrates' Association.

Ruth Morris is a former Brussels-based staff interpreter for the European Communities. She is now a freelance interpreter and translator in Israel and teaches at the School of Translation and Interpretation of Bar-Ilan University. When studying for a master's degree in communications, she came across the English case of *Iqbal Begum*, a Pakistani woman whose life sentence had been successfully appealed on the ground that she had not understood the interpreter provided at her trial. This sparked an interest in interpretation and legal processes, which led Ruth Morris to conduct research into the impact of interpreting on legal proceedings (a project based on observations at the multilingual *Demjanjuk* trial), and into the use of interpreters in a variety of English-speaking jurisdictions. She has a PhD from the Department of Law, Lancaster University.

Interpreters

and the Legal Process

Joan Colin
Ruth Morris

WATERSIDE PRESS
WINCHESTER

Interpreters and the Legal Process

Published 1996 by
WATERSIDE PRESS
Domum Road
Winchester SO23 9NN
Telephone or Fax 01962 855567
E-mail:watersidepress@compuserve.com
Online Bookstore: www.watersidepress.co.uk

First reprint 1999
Second reprint 2001

Email addresses:
Joan Colin: 100600.2701@compuserve.com
Ruth Morris: morrir@ashur.cc.biu.ac.il

ISBN Paperback 1 872 870 28 7

Cataloguing-in-publication data A catalogue record for this book can be obtained from the British Library.

Cover design John Good Holbrook Ltd, Coventry
Based on an ancient Egyptian tomb sculpture

Printing and binding Antony Rowe Ltd, Eastbourne

Print-on-demand edition First issued January 2003

For Ros, Sam, David, Michael, Jeremy and Jonathan

Foreword

It is essential that all the organizations which make up the justice system provide services which are of good quality and achieve high standards. Putting sound policies into action is a long, hard process which needs commitment, effort and resources.

In today's world, it is absolutely essential that there is, nationwide, appropriate provision of *competent* interpreting services to meet the needs of victims, witnesses and defendants caught up in the justice system. Such services must address the specific needs of local communities, as well as of the many visitors to this country.

As Lord Justice Watkins has said, proceedings involving a language-handicapped person which are conducted without assistance from an interpreter may be considered to be 'contrary to natural justice'. The authors of this book contend, correctly, that providing an interpreter who is not up to the job may also put justice in jeopardy.

We ought to be taking whatever steps are practicable to enable everyone involved in the justice process to feel confident when they handle cases involving our many diverse communities. We ought to ensure that no offence is caused through ignorance and that there is no injustice through misunderstandings.

Our system of justice is respected because it is based on public consent. We may all proclaim that we treat everyone equally and that we do not differentiate between different people. It is not enough for us to feel confident that our attitudes are all right. It is also important to *demonstrate* that the system is sensitive to the needs of our multicultural communities and foreigners.

In this book, Joan Colin and Ruth Morris have called for a professional approach to the provision of interpreting. It is now for everyone involved with the law who comes into contact with non-English speakers, limited-English speakers and deaf people to aspire to these standards. There is a need to ensure that a high-quality service is provided on an equal basis for all those who come into contact with our legal system.

Navnit Dholakia OBE, JP
June 1996

Preface and Acknowledgments

This book is written for all those people who come into contact with interpreting – for both non-English speakers and deaf people – across the legal system. We thus hope that it will be of interest to a wide range of people: judges, magistrates, lawyers, justices' clerks and court legal advisors, police officers, probation officers, prison officers, Customs and Excise officers, immigration officers and immigration appeal adjudicators, as well as administrators and managers who work alongside all these decision-makers. Last, but certainly not least, it is for interpreters, both professional and occasional.

One of our aims when writing the book was to encourage awareness of the complex issues bound up with the process of interpreting within the legal system, thereby contributing to the debate – slowly developing as the new millennium approaches – about the implications of interpreting for the proper administration of justice.

Key areas of the legal system are presented and discussed together with related interpreting issues. Items covered include procedures for entry to the United Kingdom, police investigative procedures, the work of the courts and the probation service. This approach enables linguists and non-linguists alike to understand how closely the performance of their own role depends on the practices, professionalism and attitudes of their opposite numbers. As we seek to demonstrate, where non-English speakers come into contact with the law, the interpreter – who has traditionally been seen as a mere 'mechanical adjunct' – is a vital member of the 'team' which administers justice.

Competent interpreting makes a major contribution to efficient and effective legal processes. Conversely, incompetent interpreting enhances the risk of a miscarriage of justice. We hope that everyone who reads this book will gain a greater understanding of this inescapable link between the quality of interpreting and the quality of justice.

It would be quite impossible to list all the people who have helped us by providing information, advice and support. To all of these, our thanks. A particular debt of gratitude is owed to Ellen Moerman, who has unstintingly provided invaluable insights derived from her vast experience as an interpreter and researcher. David Chandler, clerk to the Bradford justices, also deserves special mention for his exceptional support - and for bringing the two of us together.

Thanks are also due to the following people in particular:

Rosemary Abernethy	Tony Loader
Mary Brennan	Ellen Parladorio
Mary Charles	Paul Phillips
Jane Coker	Douglas Silas
Dewi Davies	Jane Shackman
Aideen Dufour	David Summers
Mary Duncan	San Hwee Tan
Steve Fieldhouse	Graham Turner
Yvonne and Malcolm Fowler	Anne-Sylvie Vassenaix
Barry Green	Michael Watkins
Nicholas Hammond	Patricia Wheeler
Barbara Lemmens	David Williamson.

We also wish to thank members of the West Midlands Probation Service and of the South Yorkshire Police.

And finally, to each other.

Joan Colin
Ruth Morris
June 1995 to January 1996

Geneva Park, Orillia, Canada
The Barn, Flaxdale House, Middleton-by-Youlgreave, England
Noah's House, Jerusalem, Israel

Interpreters and the Legal Process

CONTENTS

Glossary of Interpreting Terms

ASL: American Sign Language. The language of deaf people in the USA. It differs greatly from BSL.*

BSL: British Sign Language. The language of deaf people in the UK.*

Booth: A soundproof and ventilated enclosed space in which normally two or more simultaneous conference interpreters sit, listening to source-language material through headphones and providing interpretation in the target language over a microphone. Interpreters should have a clear view of the proceedings from the booth.

Chuchotage: see 'Whispering' below.

Community interpreter / public service interpreter / dialogue interpreter: An individual who provides interpreting services in order to enable communication between someone who does not speak the language of the service provider and a service provider within a public service or public agency framework, such as health or social services.

Conference interpreter: A conference interpreter renders verbally in one language a statement spoken in another language at a formal or informal meeting or in a conference-like situation. Professional conference interpretation may be consecutive or simultaneous regardless of the length or complexity of the original statement.

Consecutive interpretation: The interpretation is provided when the speaker has paused or completed his or her utterance.

Court interpreter: An individual who performs interpreting in a legal setting, particularly the courts.

Deaf: In this book, the word 'deaf' encompasses people who are deaf and people with impaired hearing (unless indicated otherwise in a given context).

Deafblind: People who are both deaf and blind.

Dialogue interpreter: see 'Community interpreter' above.

* For other communication methods for deaf people, see p18

Electronic interpreting: see 'Simultaneous interpreting' below.

Interpretation, interpreting; translation, translating: All these terms refer to the process of turning a message in one ('source') language into another ('target') language. The term 'translation' is used in this book where written material is re-expressed in another language in the *written* form; the term 'interpretation' (or alternatively 'interpreting') is used where material presented orally is re-expressed *orally*. 'Oral translation' is the operation in which a written text is put into another language orally, ie when the interpreter produces a sight translation. This is not the same as interpreting. The individuals who perform the linguistic operation of 'interpretation' or 'interpreting' are *interpreters*. The written operation is carried out by *translators*. Different professional skills are required for these two different functions. Court interpreters in particular may be called upon to make oral translations (sight translations) of written documents, as well as providing oral renderings (interpretation) of oral utterances.

Interpreter: A person who orally re-expresses in another language (called the 'target' language) a message uttered in the original ('source') language.

Interpreting: see 'Interpretation' above.

Interpreting techniques or modes: see 'Consecutive', 'Simultaneous', 'Whispering (*'Chuchotage'*)'.

Lipspeaker: A trained person who repeats what is said so that the deaf person can lipread more effectively.

Non-English speaker: In this book, the term 'non-English speaker' is employed to describe someone who speaks no English or only limited English.

***Per diem* interpreter:** One way of describing an interpreter who works on a daily, contract, sessional or freelance basis.

Police interpreter: An individual who performs interpreting services for the police.

Public service interpreter: see 'Community interpreter' above.

Sight translation: Orally providing a version in another language of a written text.

Sign, to sign: To use sign language.

Signing frame: A region bounded by the top of the head, the back, the space extending to elbow width on the sides, and to the hips. Signing is carried out within this frame (the whole of which must be visible to the person addressed).

Sign language: A system of communication which primarily uses manual signs and gestures. Additional information can be conveyed by using mouth patterns, the eyes and brows, the cheeks and lips, movements of the head and so on.

Simultaneous (electronic, UN-style) interpreting: The provision of an interpreted version of spoken material at the same time as the original, by an interpreter seated in a separate, soundproof booth, listening to the original through headphones and speaking into a microphone. Listeners hear the interpreted version through headphones. The interpreter should have a good view of the proceedings. In the simultaneous mode provided 'electronically', two or more interpreters work in a team, replacing each other every 20 or 30 minutes. See also the simultaneous, non-electronic mode of interpreting known as 'Whispering' or *'Chuchotage'* below.

Source language: The language of the original message or text.

Target language: The language of the interpreted or translated message or text.

Translation/translator: see 'Interpretation' above.

UN-style interpreting: see 'Simultaneous interpreting' above.

Voicing-over: When an interpreter provides a spoken-language version at the same time as a deaf person is signing (see eg p18, p41).

Whispering (*'Chuchotage'*): A 'non-electronic' form of simultaneous interpreting. The interpreted version is provided in a whisper at the same time as the original.

CHAPTER 1

Language, Communication, Interpreting and the Law

In England and Wales, as in many other countries, interpreters have become an indispensable part of the legal process. Unfortunately, many people who work in legal settings have little or no understanding of interpreting and its complexities. Not infrequently they treat interpreters with suspicion, distrust and a lack of respect for the skills which they bring to the job. It must also be acknowledged that the people engaged to interpret are not always skilled, experienced or fully competent. A central aim of this book is to encourage better understanding of the implications which attach to interpreting in this special context. Sensitivity to the items covered is essential to the proper operation of the law when the need for an interpreter arises, and ultimately to the interests of justice itself.

The following chapters seek to acquaint interpreters with aspects of the legal process, while at the same time making the relevant interpreting implications clear to legal practitioners and others. It is hoped that greater knowledge will enable everyone concerned to work more effectively. The book deals with common legal situations in which interpreters are involved. It also looks at professional standards against which expectations can be judged, as well as some lessons which might be learned from abroad. An *Epilogue* contains a historical retrospective to emphasise points made throughout the text. First, this chapter deals with a number of general points and provides an overview of certain key issues.

COMMUNICATION THROUGH LANGUAGE

Forms of language
Communication through language can take a number of forms, including spoken, written, sign and body language. At any one time, communication may involve one or more of these varieties. Written and spoken language are the forms of which people are normally most aware. Elements of language include such things as vocabulary, grammar, pronunciation, accent, word order, tone and stress.

Effective communication
When people speak, what they want to say may or may not be understood properly by the people listening to them. Speakers may take it for granted that

listeners actually understand what is said exactly as it was meant. Where there are shared assumptions, this will probably work. But where there are not, inferences – between-the-lines implications – may be missed. Throwaway references may not be picked up, and serious misunderstandings or comic repercussions may even result. The same words can mean different things to different people, as illustrated by Oscar Wilde's famous quip: 'We and the Americans have much in common, but there is always the language barrier.'

The effectiveness of communication, even between individuals who share the same language, can be affected by differences such as age, nationality, cultural background, group membership and professional status. Special uses of language include jargon, slang, mixing of expressions from languages, deliberate disguising of meaning by using code words and so on. Gestures which have one meaning in one culture, or for a particular group, may be meaningless or have a totally different meaning in another culture. Even something considered universal – such as shaking the head for 'no' and nodding for 'yes' – may be used in opposite ways in different cultures.

THE PROCESS OF INTERPRETING FROM ONE LANGUAGE TO ANOTHER

Terminology

A major theme of this book is the oral transfer of meaning between languages. The person who performs this process is called an 'interpreter', and the activity is known as 'interpreting' or 'interpretation'. This must not be confused with what lawyers call interpretation, which is a process of determining the true meaning of, say, an Act of Parliament or other written document.

The process of transferring meaning from a written text in one language to a written text in another is called 'translation'. When language professionals talk about oral translation, they mean giving an oral version of a written document. Translators and interpreters, although both involved in transferring meaning, need different skills and work in quite distinct environments.

Interpreters' skills

It is important when talking about language skills to differentiate between levels of passive and active competence. Active competence refers to the ability to make use of a language by writing or speaking it. Passive competence means being able to understand a written or spoken text well. It is possible to have a good reading knowledge of a language without being able to follow a conversation in it. For the translator, who works with written material, this may be adequate, but clearly a person who cannot follow spoken material in a particular language would not be able to do a proper job as an interpreter. The same applies to somebody who understands a language well but who cannot speak it fluently.

The skills that an interpreter needs include the ability to listen, analyse and repeat a message. Interpreters need excellent knowledge of the languages between which they are working. If they are called upon to interpret just 'one way', for example only into English, passive competence in their other language or languages might be sufficient. This is often the situation in conference interpreting, such as at the United Nations and in the European Union. In the situations referred to in this book, however, interpreters almost always have to work 'both ways', ie *into* English and *from* English. Active competence in both English and the other language is then absolutely vital.

In addition to general knowledge of a particular language, for certain assignments an interpreter must be familiar with specific aspects relating to a particular country, culture or group. In specialised settings, they will also need to know what the general subject matter of the meeting or proceedings will be, as well as the specific topics to be addressed. They will need to receive background material and to have time to prepare for the meeting, eg by studying documents.

In general interpreters need a clear voice, sharp hearing, considerable physical stamina and strong nerves. They must be able to project a confident and professional manner.

Difficulties facing interpreters

People who have no experience of trying to transfer to a second ('target') language a message expressed in another ('source') language are frequently unaware of the complexity of that process. Over the centuries, translators have tended to acquire a bad name. Interpreters are often in an even worse position, being accused by the non-professional of 'putting words' into the speaker's mouth. In court, lawyers often instruct interpreters, 'translate, don't interpret', as if 'translation' is an acceptable word-for-word activity, while 'interpreting' between two languages is the same process that lawyers engage in. In fact, because of the nature of language, word-for-word or literal translation often produces distorted communication. Translators and interpreters alike must first of all understand what the original writer or speaker meant by the combination of words used in a particular passage. Only after all the words have been understood in context can the original be expressed in the other language in a way that conveys the equivalent message.

Interpreting as a process is subject to various limitations. Because of the nature of language and the communication process, what the speaker says may be ambiguous. Even if interpreters are unsure of exactly what is meant, they may not be able to easily clarify things with the speaker. This can make it difficult to produce an accurate version of the original.

The more-or-less instant process of interpreting means that it is practically impossible for interpreters to consult reference books while working. Preparation is therefore of great importance.

On the job, the performance of an interpreter is often adversely affected by external aspects of the situation in which he or she must perform, such as the acoustics of the room, noise from outside, or the fact that the speaker is going very fast or mumbling. Interpreting quality is also influenced by internal factors such as how familiar interpreters are with the subject under discussion, how well they have been able to prepare for the specific topics on the agenda, how competent they are in the languages with which they are working and how tired they are at a particular stage, apart from generally by how good they are at interpreting.

Other difficulties confronting the interpreter may include unfamiliar words and words used in differing ways, complex grammatical constructions, unfamiliar pronunciation or mispronounced words, particulary by second-language speakers, speech defects and accents which the interpreter has difficulty understanding.

Spoken-language interpreting techniques

Technically, interpreters can choose between two main options. One is to wait until the speaker has finished, and then to deliver a version in the other language. The other is to interpret at the same time as the speaker.

Consecutive interpretation

This first technique is called 'consecutive' interpretation, because it is provided *following* the original material. If the interpreter is skilled, even long statements can be dealt with in this way. Interpreters normally take brief notes (not in shorthand) with which they can jog their memories when they give a version in the other language of what the speaker said. If the amount of material to be interpreted is short and the interpreter has a good memory, it may not be necessary to take notes. The disadvantage of the consecutive technique is that it effectively doubles the amount of time needed for a discussion, presentation or examination. The advantage is that it is possible to hear – and, when necessary, record – both original and interpretation separately. This can be very useful in order to check on accuracy. It is also relatively easy to spot inaccuracies so that these can be corrected – if somebody with the appropriate language skills is listening and able to comment.

Simultaneous interpretation

The second option is called 'simultaneous interpretation', because the material in the second language is provided by the interpreter almost instantaneously, at the same time as the original version. In its 'electronic' form, this method is used at the United Nations and the European Union, as well as many other international meetings. In these settings, interpreters sit in soundproof booths and listen through headphones to what is being said. Listeners can tune into a particular channel and hear an interpreted version through headphones.

Some interpreters prefer the consecutive technique to the simultaneous one; other interpreters hold the opposite opinion. Simultaneous interpreting does not add to the length of the proceedings. It enables any number of people to listen to interpreted versions (it is possible for an interpreted version to be provided in more than one language at any one time) without disrupting the event. It does, however, require special installations and equipment, and because of the pressure and consequent strain, it also requires at least two interpreters to share the work into any particular language. In meetings where many languages are spoken, up to four people may interpret into a given language.

Interpretation can also be provided simultaneously in another form which does not require electronic installations. It literally involves 'whispering' into someone's ear, or speaking softly so that a small number of people can follow what is being said in another language. The 'whispering' method (also known by the French term *chuchotage*) can be tiring if the interpreter must strain to hear what is being said. It may also involve sitting in uncomfortable positions for long periods of time. For organizers of events, the advantage is that it does not slow proceedings down and requires little or no investment in equipment.

Options

At times, the interpreter may use transmission equipment in order to make the interpretation *more* audible to *more* listeners. In court settings, interpreters in the USA are increasingly using some form of transmission equipment to increase efficiency and reduce strain. Often, with the court's approval, they provide the equipment on their own initiative and at their own expense.

The reader will find references to these interpreting techniques throughout this book and to circumstances in which one or other is preferred or required. Several implications stem from the interpreting technique which is selected. These range from the obvious ones of cost, time and flexibility, to such things as the interpreter's ability to identify and convey meaning implied in non-verbal forms such as facial expressions and tone of voice. For example, an interpreter unable to see a speaker's raised eyebrow may not pick up on the irony it expresses.

Modern telecommunications developments are opening up additional techniques. These include telephone interpreting and video-conferencing. However, interpreters generally prefer to be physically present in the communication situation, and a few legal and judicial practitioners have resisted the use of technology in particular cases. The future may see changes in these attitudes.

Communicating with deaf and hearing-impaired people

In Britain, there are three main methods of communication used by people who are deaf or hearing-impaired:

- British Sign Language (BSL)
- Sign-Supported English (SSE)
- lipreading.

Other less common communication methods include the Paget-Gorman sign system (PGSS), Manually Coded English (MCE), Cued Speech and Makaton Vocabulary. The sign languages used by people from outside Britain - including other English-speaking countries - differ considerably from British Sign Language and other communication methods used in Britain. For people who are both deaf and blind (known as 'deafblind'), special – non-visual – methods are used.

A number of techniques are available to people who facilitate communication between hearing people and those who are deaf or hearing-impaired: interpreting (BSL, SSE or other languages); lipspeaking, which enables lipreaders to follow what is being said efficiently; and turning sign language into spoken material (eg for telephone communication) and vice versa, or turning spoken material into written material (eg the use of a Palantype machine by a skilled operator to produce a written version of spoken material, which is then displayed on a computer screen).

Usually a BSL or SSE interpreter speaks at the same time as the deaf person signs. This is called 'voicing-over'. It is analogous to 'simultaneous interpretation' described above. Similarly, the interpreter signs as the speaker is talking.

LANGUAGE AND THE LAW

Legal language

For the outsider, the law often seems strange and forbidding. Much of this strangeness relates to legal language. Lawyers use a special form of language in understanding and applying legal concepts and arguments. In England, the language that is used for law is English, but the ordinary English-speaking person may still feel that lawyers' jargon is a rather distant cousin of everyday language. Movements such as Plain English recognise this state of affairs and make efforts to confront it.

The system of law practised in England has developed over a long period. Its current form still reflects historical aspects, such as the wearing of wigs by some lawyers and most professional judges. Another sign of the past lies in the use of Latin and French words in legal English. Until the early eighteenth century, lawyers in England believed that the law could not be administered in English! Two special languages – law Latin and law French – were used predominantly in legal proceedings for centuries, despite efforts stretching over nearly four hundred years to introduce English to the courts so that ordinary people could follow the proceedings.

Translation and interpretation in the law
Language is an inextricable part of the law. Like many other specialised fields, the law uses ordinary words in a special sense, employing jargon, foreign words and abbreviations. Quite often, a lawyer needs to explain legal matters to a non-lawyer, which involves expressing legal concepts in such a way that the lay person can grasp them. This is a kind of 'translation' process. Even among themselves, lawyers regularly have to decide on the precise meaning of a legal text. This is called 'interpretation'. These translation and interpretation processes are carried out in the same language.

The importance of words and delivery
In legal settings in particular, the exact words that people use and how they deliver them may be just as important as the gist of what they are saying. Many people are unconsciously influenced by given expressions. A witness's evaluation of a car's speed may be affected by a lawyer's choice of words such as 'smashed', 'collided', or 'brushed'. A jury's reaction may be affected by the particular term used from a range including 'baby', 'foetus', or 'product of conception' (words used in an actual case in Massachusetts). Factors such as fluency, hesitation or the use of polite expressions can affect jurors' evaluations of a witness's credibility. Lawyers can use language as a weapon in cross-examination (see Chapter 4), employing complex sentence structures, double negatives or ambiguous wording to challenge, trap, confuse and sometimes intimidate witnesses.

INTERPRETING AND THE LEGAL PROCESS

When looking at interpreting – whether for deaf people or for non-English speakers – and its impact on legal processes, several key points can be made at the outset, and these will be revisited in later chapters.

Understanding the setting
In understanding what is being said, the setting is an important factor. The interpreter must grasp the nature of various areas of the legal process, such as police interviews, court proceedings, consultations with lawyers, and assessments by probation officers. All specialised fields have their own

vocabulary. This may be full of abbreviations, foreign words, ordinary words used in a special sense, slang or code words. People not familiar with a given field will be unable to understand properly what is being said. Even if they speak the ordinary form of the language, they will need somebody to 'translate' for them. To an extent, this is what lawyers do by explaining to suspects what they are being investigated for or charged with. In order to understand the language used by people in a specialised area, outsiders must become familiar with the concepts that particular terms refer to. They also need to know the 'translation' of jargon terms.

All of this is even more true for an interpreter. In a given setting, the interpreter's task is to understand how various terms are being used, and to choose expressions in the second language in such a way as to produce the same effect that the original message would have on people who understood it directly. The degree to which this can be done varies from one situation to another. Where legal material is involved, it may be impossible to achieve this goal: because of differences between legal systems, certain concepts do not exist at all in the other language, making accurate interpretation impossible.

Differences between original and interpretation
An interpreter's use of language can never exactly parallel the message as delivered in the other language. A woman may have to 'echo' a man. A particular regional accent will be replaced with a different language variety, normally standard usage. Emphasis may have to be replaced by additional words. Like actors, who give different performances of the same role, interpreters provide different versions of the original.

The requirement to interpret 'literally' can be fraught with dangers. For example, in certain settings, if the interpreter were to reproduce all the flowery expressions used by the speaker, this might make it sound as if mockery, not deference, is intended. But to omit such terms exposes the interpreter to the charge of editing and summarising, which the 'faithful echo' is not supposed to do. Lawyers who instruct interpreters to 'translate' apparently think that word-for-word (verbatim) renderings *are* possible between two languages, and that that is what 'translation' means. They forget that every language is subject to the same problem that is acknowledged by the legal practice of 'interpretation' of texts. But at the same time they are trying to make sure that the interpreter does not 'speak for' the witness.

The interpreter's role
An interpreter who is unbiased, impartial and professional never 'speaks for' the person whose words are being put into the other language. An interpreter acts as the linguistic mouthpiece of that person. Interpreters echo the people who need their services as faithfully as they can, given the limits of language; they do not

replace them. They certainly do not act as their advocates, nor do they give legal advice (see, generally, Chapter 7, *Professional Standards*).

This does not mean, however, that interpreters function as nothing but a sophisticated 'echo machine'. Interpreters must always be on the alert for possible misunderstandings. These may occur because neither party is aware that aspects of the other's cultural background have not been understood correctly. Similarly, listeners may not have grasped the implications of what has been said in the other language, although these would have been clear to a person who speaks that language and comes from the same country or group. There are no clear-cut rules for interpreters about how to act under these circumstances. They have to deal with the communication issues and any resulting dilemmas as they see fit.

The impact of the interpreter

Proceedings without an interpreter differ in many ways from those where interpretation services are provided. But the degree to which proceedings are affected – adversely or otherwise – by the fact that interpretation is occurring varies immensely.

The key concept should be quality. Engaging unskilled people to provide interpreting services means building a weak link into the legal process. The quality of an interpreter's performance is not limited to the number of mistakes made. Whether deliberately or inadvertently, the interpreter may use more (or less) polite language than the original; inject or omit hesitation; use more formal or less formal language; eliminate or introduce ambiguities. These and other language choices influence the proceedings in many subtle ways. A suspect or witness may become more cooperative or less so depending on the interpreter's use of language. Incompetent interpretation can mislead a witness. Interaction between the interpreter and a lawyer may, for example, cause a jury to lose sympathy with the lawyer.

Competent interpreting, on the other hand, makes proceedings more efficient. Without controlling what is being said, an experienced interpreter may draw attention to relevant cultural issues and avoid misunderstandings. The right choice of technique and its skilled application can speed things along and save time, resources and money. With good interpreters, proceedings involving people who need linguistic assistance are not the nightmare that they can become with incompetent interpreting.

Aspects related to the provision of a linguistic link by an interpreter can affect the proceedings. Thus, an interpreter may interrupt in order to request clarification, or to ask for somebody to slow down or speak up. Other people in the proceedings may comment on the fact that an interpreter is present. They may comment on aspects of the interpreter's performance. All of this draws attention to the interpreter.

The very presence of an interpreter in a particular situation may change the way in which people communicate. People have a natural tendency to address their comments to the interpreter, not to the person to whom they are supposed to be speaking. When the interpreter is standing or sitting right next to the non-English speaking person, this may give the undesirable impression of a private conversation - something that the competent interpreter will avoid.

Sign language and the legal process

The nature of sign language makes sign-language interpreters particularly visible. In addition, they may need more information than is normally available. For example, in order to interpret the sentence 'he opened the window' into British Sign Language (BSL), the precise type of window must be known – sash, casement, sliding, louvered, horizontal or vertical pivoting, and so on. If the window has been broken, the interpreter may need to know *how* it was broken: with a stone, boot, fist and so on. Unless special arrangements are made, this information may only become available at a later stage. Without it, the interpreter will be forced to guess. The result may be inaccurate interpretation, leading to incorrect responses. A witness may be made to look evasive or untruthful because the interpreter had insufficient information to do a good job.

Quality in interpreting

Interpreters work under considerable pressure and, unlike translators, without the possibility of first producing a draft version and correcting it. Inevitably, mistakes are made, even by highly skilled individuals. In court, where the record of the proceedings consists in part of the interpreter's words, that record will not be totally reliable. Testimony (ie oral evidence) and questioning will suffer.

If the proceedings last more than 30-50 minutes, engaging two interpreters will contribute to better quality because the interpreters can take turns. They will not have to work when tired and so they will make fewer errors. Additionally, the interpreter who is not on duty can monitor the other's performance and draw attention to any significant mistakes in the interpretation. Discussions about what the witness really said and appeals on the grounds of incompetent interpreting are costly matters. In complex or lengthy proceedings, the extra cost of the second interpreter will be more than offset by time saved and mistakes avoided.

An interpreter who receives an assignment should have some familiarity with the general area and specific subject matter. Codes of ethics issued by various associations of professional interpreters often require their members to accept only those jobs which they are competent to handle (see, generally, Chapter 7, *Professional Standards*). Overall or general familiarity with a relatively wide area (such as 'legal' or 'medical' interpreting) is not enough to guarantee competent performance on a particular assignment. Interpreters must be given an opportunity to refresh their memories, and to prepare for the engagement. They need to study specific topics and familiarise themselves in both languages with the terminology that is likely to be used. For example, evidence may be presented about a document, or about a bullet, or about blood. The interpreter will need to read background material on document analysis, ballistics, and DNA testing. Interpreters who are well prepared do a better job. The quality of justice benefits.

CHAPTER 2

Interpreters and the Police

PART I: DEALING WITH SUSPECTS

There are forty-three police forces in England and Wales and their main aims, as outlined in the government white paper, *Police Reform: A Police Service for the Twenty-first Century* (HMSO, 1993), are 'to fight and prevent crime; uphold the law; bring to justice those who break the law; protect, help and reassure the community, and to provide good value for money'. In order to achieve each of these aims it is frequently necessary for police officers to rely on the services of an interpreter. Many cities and towns have a great diversity of cultures and languages. European obligations have led to greater freedom of movement within member states, with a consequent increase in the number of non-English speakers involved in criminal offences. There are also significant numbers of deaf people being arrested who need the expert assistance of a sign-language interpreter.

The police are becoming more aware of culture-based issues that may affect the willingness of victims or witnesses to report incidents or to respond to questioning and give evidence. Education programmes for young people are going some way towards breaking down the suspicions and barriers. The recruitment of bilingual police officers from local communities is another way forward and there are schemes for police to receive training in languages other than English. Language skills can be useful at the scene of an accident if someone has been injured, or in the early stages of an investigation. But it is unwise for officers who have language ability but no interpreting skills to assume that they can satisfactorily replace a competent interpreter.

The Police and Criminal Evidence Act 1984 (PACE), which governs the investigation of crime and the treatment of suspects, and the accompanying Codes of Practice (the latest version was promulgated in 1995), introduced procedures designed to provide clearly defined rights for those people suspected of crime and detained at police stations for questioning. These rights include the right to inform someone else that they are under arrest; a right of access to free legal advice; and the right to consult the PACE Codes of Practice. The Codes regulate a range of activities including police powers to 'stop and search', to search premises, to seize property, the detention, treatment and questioning of people by police officers, and the tape-recording of interviews at police stations. A breach of the Codes may result in a court ruling that related evidence (for example in relation to a police interview) is inadmissible (see *R v Van Axel and Wezer* (1991)).

Non-English speakers and deaf people
PACE Code C outlines the action to be taken by a police officer if a detained person does not speak or understand English, or if the suspect is deaf:

> ... unless Annex C [which relates to urgent interviews] applies, a person must not be interviewed in the absence of a person capable of acting as an interpreter if:
>
> (a) he has difficulty in understanding English;
> (b) the interviewing officer cannot himself speak the person's own language; and
> (c) the person wishes an interpreter to be present. (Code C, para 12.2)

And in relation to special groups:

> If the person appears to be deaf or there is doubt about his hearing or speaking ability or ability to understand English, and the custody officer cannot establish effective communication, the custody officer must as soon as practicable, call an interpreter and ask him to provide the information required above. (Code C, para 13.2)

Register of interpreters
To ensure effective compliance with PACE requirements, most police forces maintain a register of interpreters. However, the data held, and the way it is compiled and administered, can vary. A survey commissioned in 1992 by the Nuffield Interpreter Project showed that of the 43 police forces, 41 maintained some sort of register. It also showed that whilst most registers recorded personal details such as the name, address, telephone number and languages spoken by the interpreter, only a minority included information such as the ability to translate as well as to interpret (see Chapter 1), and details of professional qualifications. In addition, the survey identified the existence of wide variations in the methods used for the selection and subsequent monitoring of interpreters.

Police registers of interpreters are generally held on a force's central computer system which can be accessed through divisional control rooms. The information held is covered by data protection legislation and is confidential, although other public services such as the courts, probation service and Crown Prosecution Service can be provided with such information. Some local initiatives have, with the permission of the interpreters involved, resulted in the data being made available to other public agencies to enable them to develop their own registers.

Occasions can arise when it is necessary to refer to alternative interpreter services, for example in the case of a rare language, or to assist in the preliminary stages when identifying the language spoken, or to inform suspects of their rights when it is not possible to call out an interpreter on a police force's own register. To overcome such difficulties, a search of neighbouring police lists will be carried out, or a commercial agency contacted, to find an appropriate interpreter. When outside agencies are used it is more difficult to exercise quality control.

In addition telephone interpreter services can be used for preliminary matters. Three-way telephone links or conference facilities should be set up when using this type of service to enable each of the people involved to hear what is being said. Telephone interpreting (see pp133-134) is normally a stop-gap or 'first aid' solution only.

There are a number of specialist registers, such as the directory produced by the Council for the Advancement of Communication with Deaf People (CACDP), the National Register and the membership list of the Association of Police and Court Interpreters. Official guidance is found in Home Office Circular 88/1985. This says that, in order to be proficient, the interpreter must:

(1) be able to understand, speak, read and write English and the other language to a level of competence which will include the specialised terms and procedures which may be encountered in police interviews as well as the vocabulary of normal conversation. It is important, for example, that the interpreter fully understands the meanings of the different types of offence and concepts such as 'caution' and 'bail';
(2) be familiar with both cultural backgrounds;
(3) be able to interpret and translate accurately;
(4) act in an impartial professional manner and respect confidentiality.

Guidelines

Several police forces have produced information and guidelines for interpreters on their lists. Some also provide information for police officers on how to work with an interpreter. The South Yorkshire Police *Notes of Guidance for Interpreters and Police Officers* recognise the skills required. The opening passage states: 'It is appreciated that accurate interpreting in any context is a demanding task which requires a high level of linguistic and professional skills.' Later there is a note for police officers asking them to:

... please remember that the Interpreters are often professional people with advanced linguistic skills and qualifications and they should be treated accordingly. Without their expertise, communication with the non-English speaking public would be almost impossible. During lengthy interviews of suspects or witnesses, police officers should ensure a break is given, where possible, every hour, to allow the interpreter a short break or rest.

The notes make clear the responsibilities that administrators and police officers have in ensuring that interpreters receive appropriate support throughout an assignment – and that payment of the interpreter is expedited.

Guidelines can also serve as a useful source of reference for interpreters: they often explain police procedures for interviewing suspects and witnesses, and include examples of forms, such as witness statements and the notice to someone whose interview has been tape-recorded. Some guidelines explicitly recognise the independent status of interpreters and indicate the ethical behaviour expected of them. An example from the *Metropolitan Police Handbook* reads:

Avoid:
- becoming personally involved in an investigation
- assisting prisoners, witnesses or victims
- having contact with anyone involved in a case (this includes families, witnesses, solicitors, etc, as well as the person you are actually interpreting for) other than in an official context or giving them your home address or telephone number. If any approaches are made to you, this should be reported to the officer in the case.

Criminal investigations
The stages generally followed during an investigation into a criminal offence are as follows:

- allegation/report of a crime
- investigation
- arrest
- arrival at the police station
- pre-interview
- interview
- post-interview.

There are occasions when interpreters are needed for the early stages of an investigation, possibly to assist in enquiries at the scene of a crime or road traffic incident, but generally they are called to a police station after a suspect has been arrested.

Contacting the interpreter
PACE and the Codes of Practice include provisions concerning the length of time that someone can be detained at a police station, and deal with how he or she is to be treated. Time limits place pressures on the police to obtain the

services of an interpreter speedily and efficiently. During the initial telephone call the police officer should ascertain whether the interpreter's language and translation skills are appropriate for the assignment. Valuable time will be lost if, on arrival at the police station, a different interpreter has to be located. It is helpful if officers provide information about technical matters which might arise, so that the interpreter can take reference works to the interview, eg an appropriate dictionary or glossary.

Interpreters are often called out at night to attend an investigation. In these circumstances it is important that the caller gives the interpreter clear instructions on how to find the venue and details such as parking arrangements, and what to do on arrival. An interpreter should not be expected to wait in a queue at the front desk of a police station.

Arrival at the police station

If the suspect has not been able to communicate with anyone by the time the interpreter arrives, he or she may be in a distressed or confused state. The police officer should explain that the interpreter is an independent professional whose services will be free of charge. The manner in which these preliminary items are dealt with can set the tone for all that follows.

In the presence of the police officer, the interpreter should hold a brief conversation with the person who has been arrested to confirm compatibility of language and dialect and to make sure that there are no political, gender or other barriers which might significantly affect the communication process. It is vital that the interpreter does not allow this discussion to touch on aspects of the arrest and investigation. If matters like this are raised, the interpreter should remind the suspect that everything said will be interpreted to the police officer. Once these preliminary items are completed the formal procedures for dealing with a suspect will take place in front of the police custody officer (the 'custody sergeant').

Unless time is very short, there should be a briefing meeting between the investigating officer and interpreter about how the interview will be conducted. It is standard practice for the interpreter's role to be clarified by the investigating officer at the preliminary preparation and planning stage, thereby avoiding this being dealt with whilst the interview is taking place.

Pre-interview

At the time of an arrest police officers must tell people why they are being arrested and caution them (see under next heading). Even if suspects *appear* to have understood at the time why they are being arrested, it should not be assumed that non-English speakers, hearing-impaired or deaf people really do understand all that is said. These pre-interview procedures, which are repeated at the police station for all suspects, should be conducted through an interpreter.

Caution

The custody officer will give the reasons for the arrest, and caution the suspect, before reading his or her statutory rights. The caution (as amended in 1994) is:

You do not have to say anything but it may harm your defence if you do not mention when questioned something which you later rely on in court. Anything you do say may be given in evidence.

It is the responsibility of the police officer to ensure that the wording and effect of the caution are understood. The implications of this caution are legally complex. Interpreting the caution accurately into another language can prove tricky. Police officers should be aware of this and be prepared to explain in plain English what the caution says and what it means. In particular, the phrases 'may harm your defence' and 'later rely on', may be difficult concepts to transfer from English into another language.

Rights

The statutory rights of detained people are then read to them:

You have the right to:
1. Speak to an independent solicitor free of charge
2. Have someone told that you have been arrested
3. Consult the Codes of Practice covering police powers and procedures.
   You may do any of these things now, but if you do not, you may still do so at any other time whilst detained at the police station.

The officer responsible for preliminary matters should ensure, through the interpreter, that the detained person really does understand these rights. It should be realised that the offer of free legal advice and an impartial interpreter may even create suspicion in the mind of a detainee accustomed to a repressive or totalitarian regime. When the rights have been explained, the custody officer will say:

You can do any of these things now or, if you do not want to now, you can at any time during your detention at the police station. Do you want to speak to a solicitor?

The next question will be:

Do you want anyone informed?

Finally, the suspect is asked to sign the custody record to confirm that he or she has been read his or her rights. Whether or not the person agrees to sign, an interpreter will be asked to confirm, by signing the document, that these rights have been interpreted.

Notices

The suspect is then handed copies of a 'Notice to Detained Person' and 'Notice of Entitlements'. The Home Office has made translations in a number of languages available to police forces throughout England and Wales. The 'Notice to Detained Person' includes the three rights already mentioned, together with some additional details about each and an explanation of what is meant by free legal advice. The 'Notice of Entitlements' summarises selected parts of each of the main PACE Codes of Practice. It includes information about the contents for citizens of independent Commonwealth countries or foreign nationals who wish to communicate with their high commission, embassy or consulate and receive private visits from a consular officer, to talk to or to arrange for legal advice (*R v Bassil and Mouffareg* (1990)).

Whilst these notices have been translated into other languages, the PACE Codes are only available in English. Where possible, suspects should be given time to read through the notices and to ask for clarification. The interpreter must be prepared to sight-translate when required. This could be a time-consuming task for both the interpreter and the non-English speaker because the terminology in both notices is complex and the contents are difficult for even a native English speaker to understand.

If there is sufficient evidence at this stage for the suspect to be charged with an offence (sometimes called 'putting the charge'), the custody officer will follow the procedures described on p37.

Implementing the rights

An interpreter may make a telephone call or write a letter on a suspect's behalf if they cannot manage it themselves. If contact with a high commission, embassy or consulate has to be made, the interpreter should ask the custody officer for specific instructions. The suspect will also be advised that the contents of a letter or information given over the telephone will be noted and might be given in evidence. This does not apply to any communications with a solicitor concerning the investigation which are privileged and thus confidential. There are a variety of ways in which a suspect can obtain a solicitor. A specific solicitor might already be known to the suspect, or a telephone call to a friend or relative might be made. Otherwise the duty solicitor service will be contacted by the police, or a solicitor may be identified from a list of solicitors maintained at the police station.

Duty solicitor

There are certain obligations on duty solicitors under the 'Legal Aid Board Duty Solicitor Arrangements 1990'. For example:

(i) A duty solicitor shall provide initial advice by speaking directly to the suspect on the telephone unless he/she is in or adjacent to the police station and can immediately advise the suspect in person.

(ii) The duty solicitor shall attend the suspect if any of these circumstances apply ('qualifying circumstances'):

   (a) the suspect has been arrested in connection with an arrestable offence and the police intend to interview him/her; or

   (b) the police intend to resolve an issue of identification by parade, group, film, video or confrontation; or

   (c) the suspect complains of serious maltreatment by the police.

It is up to a solicitor to exercise discretion as to whether or not to attend. The decision will be based on whether advice can satisfactorily be given by telephone. If the solicitor is to attend for the interview, nothing much can be done at the police station by the interpreter until the solicitor arrives. In the meantime, the police officer should ensure that the interpreter and the suspect are not left alone together.

Solicitors and interpreters

A solicitor might bring an interpreter along for this part of the proceedings or the solicitor might speak the same language as the suspect, but these instances are rare compared with occasions when the interpreter who has been appointed by the police will also be required to interpret for the private conference between the solicitor and the suspect. Everything that the interpreter hears being said between solicitor and suspect is covered by the same privilege applicable to what a suspect says to his or her lawyer (*Du Barré v Livette* (1791), and see below, *Conferences between solicitor and client*). This is referred to in the South Yorkshire Police *Notes of Guidance*:

> Everything said between a solicitor and client is confidential and therefore inadmissible in evidence. If an interpreter is required to assist a solicitor by translating, this is one occasion when no record need be made. *That conversation must not be discussed with anyone.* (emphasis in original)

On arrival at the police station the solicitor speaks to the custody officer and investigating officer, to confirm details about the police investigation. The solicitor should also speak to the person engaged by the police to act as interpreter, in order to confirm that the individual comprehends the interpreter's role, speaks and understands the language and dialect of the suspect, and is impartial. Issues concerning the solicitor's duty of confidence to the client might be clarified, together with the implications for the interpreter of legal privilege. Some solicitors, particularly those whose work brings them into regular contact with local ethnic communities, understand how to work with interpreters, but there are many who have little or no experience of communicating with non-English speakers or with deaf people.

Conferences between solicitor and client

At this stage, a shift occurs in the dynamics of the interpreting situation. Interpreter-solicitor-suspect relationships are different from those between the interpreter, police officer and suspect. Solicitor-client interviews can be highly charged occasions requiring skilful management by the solicitor. The fact that the suspect does not speak English or is deaf can exacerbate an already stressful environment. The solicitor can help the interview along by following certain strategies such as:

- avoiding inappropriate linguistic levels
- establishing a rapport with the suspect
- reaffirming the impartial and confidential position of the interpreter
- concentrating on the issues to be addressed in the police interview.

During the private conference the solicitor listens to the suspect's explanation of events leading up to the arrest. If the suspect is not known to the solicitor, some time will be taken up eliciting personal details and identifying relevant information. Aspects of PACE may need further clarification. Eligibility for legal aid if matters are to go to court, and other immediate issues such as the evidence collected by the police, will have to be checked. The implications of the caution, such as answering the officer's questions or remaining silent, will be addressed.

The solicitor should do everything possible to avoid misunderstandings and aim to create a supportive, non-judgemental atmosphere. Straightforward sentences should be used, avoiding complex and idiomatic language as far as possible. It is important to explain in simple terms what words such as 'bail' and 'remand' mean. The responsibility for doing this lies with the solicitor and not with the interpreter. The solicitor-client conference provides an opportunity for the solicitor to identify any additional disabilities that the suspect might have, such as diminished hearing, mental disorder or handicap (see p38 under the heading *Appropriate adult*). Because of their linguistic skills, interpreters are more likely to notice signs of mental disorder in a deaf or non-English speaker than other people who come into contact with suspects. If this should happen at the police station, the interpreter should notify the custody officer and solicitor immediately.

THE POLICE INTERVIEW

Procedures for the conduct of police interviews are clearly defined in the PACE Codes of Practice. These are also detailed in *The Interviewer's Rule Book* (see p38 below) and *A Guide to Interviewing*, produced by the National Investigative Interviewing Research and Development Project Team with contributions from lawyers, researchers and psychologists, as well as police officers. At the time of writing (1996), both publications are being revised into a single volume. Police interview techniques and the rules for recording suspects' statements have been radically overhauled since the mid-1980s, with a move towards greater accountability on the part of interviewers.

Interview rooms are normally small. In order to avoid distractions during the interview, they are bare apart from necessities such as a table, seating and tape-recording equipment. Interviews are invariably tape-recorded, which makes those involving interpreters less tedious and time-consuming than when there was a requirement for everything said in both languages to be written down. However, people tend to speak at the same time, as well as before the last question or answer has been fully interpreted. This creates problems for the interpreter, as it does later on for the listener and transcriber.

When everyone is in the interview room, the police officer loads the tape recorder with fresh tapes. Once the machine has started recording the officer reads a formal introduction which identifies each person present, including the interpreter. The caution (p31) is repeated, and the interview starts. It is sensible to ask every individual whose voice is going to be heard on the tape to introduce themselves at this stage. It can be difficult identifying voices on a tape-recording, particularly if several people are speaking and the evidence is heard months later.

When the interview is conducted via an interpreter, an accurate record of everything said in both languages is tape-recorded, including 'explanatory' items between the interpreter and suspect or officer, and not just the questions asked and answers given. During the interview, the officer may comment, for the record, on 'non-verbal' behaviour by the suspect, such as nodding or shaking of the head. Whether or not these movements are subsequently understood correctly might depend on the police officer recognising their true implication in a given cultural context. For example, in some cultures a shake of the head can mean 'yes'. Similarly, deaf people tend to nod during 'signing' to indicate that the message is coming across. If a solicitor is present, comments by the interviewing officer can be monitored. If necessary they can be contradicted or challenged by the solicitor whilst the tape is running.

35

At the conclusion of the interview, and before the recorder is switched off, the suspect will be handed a 'Notice to Suspect' which explains the use which will be made of the tape-recording, and the arrangements for access to it. This notice must be translated orally by the interpreter as it requires the suspect to indicate whether he or she wishes to receive a copy of the tape or whether it is to be sent to his or her solicitors. The notice is then signed by the suspect who will also be asked to sign the label which is used to seal the master tape; this too should be translated by the interpreter. For security reasons, the interpreter's address must not be written on the label. To conclude matters:

> the police officer shall make a note in his notebook of the fact that the interview has taken place and has been recorded on tape, its time, duration and date and the identification number of the master tape. (Code E, para 5.1)

The interpreter and the interviewing officer will each make a written statement, in English giving details such as the date, time and place where the interview was held and stating that it was conducted through an interpreter.

Written record of tape-recorded interview
For pragmatic reasons the courts have accepted that, on the whole, a summary of a tape-recorded interview can be produced to the court and be proved as secondary evidence of the interview, subject to certain precautions (*R v Rampling* (1987)). In the case of tape-recorded interviews, what is frequently referred to as the 'record of interview' is in fact such a *summary* (Baldwin and Bedward, Crim LR [1991] 671).

> Any summary of the interview should be made by the officer in English. It is *not* the interpreter's responsibility to prepare the written summary. (*Metropolitan Police Handbook for Interpreters*, 1994)

Similarly, an interpreter should not be involved in decisions about what is to be included in any written 'record of interview' or 'summary of interview'.

Written record of interview which has not been tape-recorded
There are now relatively few occasions when interviews have to be taken down in writing instead of by audio-cassette. It is a time-consuming method because the interviewing officer has to write down every question and answer in English and the interpreter has to do the same in the suspect's language (form MG 13). After the interview, the interpreter translates the whole foreign-language record into English. When this is completed the interpreter makes a witness statement giving details of the time, place and identification of the original written interview.

36

The interpreter will then make a witness statement (which may become a court exhibit) setting out the procedure used and producing both statements with exhibit labels, and the original interview record in the foreign language. Finally, the interpreter reads through the officer's notes of the translated replies and initials them to confirm that they are an accurate record.

Post-interview

If there is no basis for a charge at this stage the suspect will be released unless the police decide to apply to a magistrates' court for a warrant to further detain the suspect (something which in practice occurs only in relation to very serious offences). Otherwise the suspect may be bailed to return to a police station on some future date for inquiries to continue. When the police decide that there *is* sufficient evidence to prosecute, the suspect will either be:

- charged with an offence and released on police bail to attend court; or
- charged with the offence and kept in police custody to appear before a court; or
- released - and reported for a summons to be considered by a senior officer.

When a suspect is charged, the interpreter is expected to sign a record of the caution having been given, and of anything that person says in response. A written charge sheet is then issued to that person, including details of the offence and the relevant legal provisions. This document contains important information which the officer will bring to the person's attention through the interpreter. The interpreter may be asked to translate some or all of the material.

Remands and bail

Any necessary decisions will then be made by the custody officer about whether to grant bail to the accused person or to keep him or her in custody pending early appearance before a magistrates' court: see *Remands and Bail*, pp102-103. The interpreter will need to convey what is said to the accused person in this regard, including explanations, grounds or reasons given by the custody officer and any bail conditions.

Role of the Crown Prosecution Service

After a suspect has been charged by the police, decisions relating to prosecution normally become the responsibility of the Crown Prosecution Service (CPS), ie CPS lawyers. The Introduction to the *Code for Crown Prosecutors* states:

> The decision to prosecute an individual is a serious step. Fair and effective prosecution is essential to the maintenance of law and order. But even in a

small case, a prosecution has serious implications for all involved - the victim, a witness and a defendant . . . (para 1.1)

and under 'General Principles':

The duty of the Crown Prosecution Service is to make sure that the right person is prosecuted for the right offence and that all relevant facts are given to the court. (para 2.2)

SOME FURTHER INTERPRETING ISSUES

In addition to the procedures described so far in this chapter are those which involve special groups of people, such as juveniles or mentally disordered suspects. There are also complex procedures associated with the identification of suspects or which, because of the nature of the offence under investigation, involve experts such as police surgeons or other forensic experts. Matters such as these raise further issues for the interpreter. Whilst they deserve full consideration it is not possible to elaborate on them here, but they are referred to briefly in the following notes.

Appropriate adult

If the suspect is under 18 years of age (ie a 'juvenile' or 'youth'), an appropriate adult should attend the interview: this can be a parent, guardian, relative, social worker or another responsible adult aged 18 or over who is not a police officer or employed by the police. Other vulnerable categories of people qualify to have an appropriate adult with them when interviewed. The mentally disordered or mentally handicapped are also protected by provisions in the PACE Codes.

The *Interviewer's Rule Book (Investigative Interviewing)* (Home Office Central Planning Unit, HMSO, 1992) explains the role of an appropriate adult as follows:

- to advise the interviewee;
- to observe whether the interview is being conducted properly and fairly;
- to ease and assist the communication between the officer and the person being interviewed so that both understand what each is saying.
  Appropriate adults are not to be there simply as an observer. They may, for example, need to interrupt questioning to check that the interviewee properly understands what is being said, or that an answer is not misrepresented by the officer. The officer must appreciate this role and ensure the appropriate adult also understands.

This guidance gives an appropriate adult the opportunity to be involved in the interview in such a way that the task of managing the interview becomes more complex. The interviewing officer has to be careful to ensure that control of the speakers is maintained so that the resulting tape-recording is audible and clearly identifies who is talking to whom.

People not under arrest
Sometimes a person goes voluntarily to a police station to assist with an investigation. In these circumstances, the person must be told that:

• they are not under arrest
• they are free to leave if they wish
• they are entitled to free legal advice.

If the person is deaf, hearing-impaired or a non-English speaker, precautions should be taken to ensure that effective communication takes place.

Formal caution
When the police have evidence sufficient to charge a suspect who has also admitted guilt, they have a discretion to issue a formal caution instead of bringing court proceedings. A caution in this sense is a formal warning given by a senior police officer in uniform, normally at a police station. It is used extensively for minor offences, particularly in the case of young offenders. The caution will usually be given at some later date. It is feasible that an interpreter may be required, not for the offender, but for an accompanying person, such as a parent or guardian.

Search
When suspects are first brought to a police station it may be necessary for them to be searched. This should only be carried out after the officer has explained, through the interpreter, why the police want to conduct the search and what is involved.

Doctor
If a doctor is called to the police station, an interpreter may be required to interpret for both the doctor and the suspect. The interpreter should also be aware that if, at any time while a suspect is in custody, that person informs the interpreter that he or she feels unwell or is injured, the interpreter must immediately pass that information on to the officer concerned.

Drink-drive specimen procedure

The law allows breath test procedures to be carried out without an interpreter being present. However, the courts have ruled that if people have not understood what is involved in a procedure, they cannot be found to have refused to cooperate (the 'mental processes' argument as applied to warnings and non-English speakers: see *Beck v Sager* (1979)).

Identification procedures

Further details about identification procedures are outlined in *Part III* of this chapter: *Witnesses and Victims.*

Other agencies of law enforcement

Among the many other agencies of law enforcement which have an investigative or prosecution function are the following:

- Customs and Excise (see Chapter 3)
- Serious Fraud Office
- Health and Safety Executive
- TV Licence Records Office
- local authorities
- National Society for the Prevention of Cruelty to Children
- Royal Society for the Prevention of Cruelty to Animals.

Often the staff of these agencies have little active experience of relevant communications issues such as are specifically addressed in police guidelines and codes; nor do they have any ready way of obtaining an interpreter for communication with non-English speakers or deaf people.

PART II: COMMUNICATION AND INTERPRETERS

This part of Chapter 2 looks at specific issues in relation to communicating with non-English speakers, deaf and hearing-impaired people during police interviews. The term 'non-English speakers' is used here as an abbreviated way of referring to people who speak no English or limited English. The term 'deaf people' is used here as an abbreviated way of referring to people who are deaf or who have impaired hearing.

PACE Codes of Practice

Two paragraphs of Code C (3.6;13.2) require police officers to be aware of communication issues in relation to people detained and questioned if:

- there are language, hearing or speech difficulties

- the interviewing officer cannot speak the person's own language
- the custody officer cannot establish effective communication
- the person wishes an interpreter to be present
- there is doubt about the person's ability to understand English
- there is doubt about the person's speaking ability
- the person appears to be deaf
- there is doubt about the person's hearing ability.

There are also issues concerning effective communication with an appropriate adult (see p38), who may be a parent, guardian or other individual, if:

- an appropriate adult appears to be deaf
- there is doubt about an appropriate adult's hearing ability
- there is doubt about an appropriate adult's speaking ability.

The Code makes it necessary for police officers to determine whether a non-English speaker or a deaf person needs an interpreter. An individual may understand some English, and may speak some English – but may not be able to understand *enough* or speak *well enough* for the purposes of:

- understanding the rights as they are read out .
- understanding questions in interview (words, concepts and implications)
- understanding and responding appropriately to the assumptions underlying requests, questions, procedures or explanations
- reacting at a 'normal' speed to questions or requests
- reacting as 'normal' to questions or requests
- using 'normal' body language (eg looking directly at an authority figure, or not, as appropriate in own culture)
- expressing themselves in a way likely to sound coherent, convincing, plausible
- in the case of an appropriate adult, having the linguistic competence (understanding and speaking) to be able to intervene when and as effectively as an English speaker would.

To summarise, relevant issues include:

- who assesses the need for an interpreter?
- on what basis?
- is a reading or comprehension test to be applied?
- if so, who is responsible for drawing up the test?
- who will obtain the services of the interpreter?
- what qualifications should the person who is to act as interpreter have?

By using a competent interpreter, some of the aspects listed above can be resolved. There are documented instances where neither police officers nor the non-English speaker realized that effective communication was not taking place. This puts the police officer in a difficult position, because unless it appears to him or her 'that a person does not understand what the caution means', he or she is highly unlikely to 'go on to explain it in his own words' (as should be done according to Note for Guidance 4C to Code E). Yet it might later be successfully argued in court that the person had not understood the caution (*Beck v Sager* referred to on p40). On the other hand, it has also been held that if police officers are *not aware* that somebody is deaf, it is not possible to show that there has been a breach of PACE provisions. However, if during an interview an officer begins to have *doubts* about the suspect's hearing ability, the courts have ruled that it would be a breach of the PACE provisions to continue with the interview. If it were shown later that a person had impaired hearing, the interview would be inadmissible as evidence under PACE (*R v Clarke* (1982)).

Code C of PACE, para 10.5B (which deals with 'special warnings' under the Criminal Justice and Public Order Act 1994 concerning refusal to account for certain matters) also acknowledges the need to achieve communication and at times for this purpose to use 'ordinary language'. Communication difficulties do not occur *solely* in connection with non-English speakers and hearing-impaired and deaf people.

Code E of PACE, para 4.4, provides for the police officer to take a contemporaneous note of the interview where the suspect is deaf or there is doubt about his or her hearing ability, in addition to tape-recording it. However, many deaf people have low-level literacy skills and may not be able to read the officer's notes. The *only* way to obtain an accurate record of an interpreted interview with a deaf person is to video the entire interview, in order to show the signing frame (see *Glossary*) of both the interpreter and the deaf suspect.

OBTAINING AN INTERPRETER

Paragraph 13.2 of Code C refers to 'a person capable of acting as an interpreter', but no guidance is given as to what this means. Home Office Circular 88/1985, referred above (p28), contains more specific guidance on interpreter proficiency. Officers who have to contact an interpreter should be familiar with the content and implications of the circular. Note for Guidance 3D refers to a list of interpreters having 'the necessary skills and experience' in police interviews, thereby indicating the need to obtain a *competent* interpreter.

The only references to *obtaining* the services of an interpreter appear in para 13.1 of Code C (see Note for Guidance 3D). The revised version of the Codes (1995) retains the original text of Note 3D, which suggests contacting social services departments for a list of interpreters for the deaf. It also refers to the local Community Relations Council as a source of interpreters for non-English speakers. These suggestions are out of date and incomplete: see next section.

Contacting the right person

Assuming that it has been decided that the non-English speaker does need an interpreter, the correct language and dialect must then be identified. If there is any doubt, it is advisable to make absolutely sure of the correct identification before calling out an interpreter. It may be possible to do this preliminary checking over the telephone, by calling a qualified individual interpreter or a reputable telephone interpreting service. It will obviously be necessary for the interpreter to speak to the non-English speaker directly in order to check on language match. This approach is not available in the case of deaf people. As indicated in Chapter 1, in Britain three main methods of communication are used by people who are deaf or hearing-impaired:

- British Sign Language (BSL)
- Sign-Supported English (SSE)
- lipreading.

It is necessary to determine whether to call a BSL or SSE (or other) interpreter, or whether a lipspeaker is needed. Only then can the appropriate person be contacted. When referring to any register of interpreters in order to find an appropriate interpreter, it is vital to refer to explanatory notes and check the entries carefully.

The role of the interpreter at the police station

Paragraph 13.10 of Code C refers to making arrangements for an interpreter 'to explain as soon as practicable the offence concerned and any other information given by the custody officer'. This may give a misleading impression. The explanations and information must come directly from the officer. Communication is then *facilitated* by the interpreter. An exception to this rule is when the interpreter may be asked to make a telephone call or write a letter on a suspect's behalf to those people, such as a consul, mentioned on p32. A custody officer may need to provide 'very specific instructions' when the interpreter has to contact an official body on behalf of the detained person.

COMMUNICATION DURING INTERVIEW

Police officers are in charge of conducting any interview; interpreters have the primary responsibility for the accuracy and completeness of the communication facilitated by them. It is advisable for police officers to check with the interpreter before beginning an interview that the arrangements are suitable for effective communication. There are a number of practical issues specific to police interviews. Some of the same points also apply when a non-English speaker or hearing-impaired person is interviewed without an interpreter if the police officer and interviewee think that they can manage without the services of an interpreter.

Preliminaries

Seating arrangements must be appropriate for communication between all three parties (police officer, interviewee, interpreter or lipspeaker). This involves a number of issues, including:

- positioning
- lighting - there should be plenty of light on the sign-language interpreter, but he or she should not be placed in front of a window or with light coming from behind as this darkens the face. The same applies to the interviewee who is communicating in sign language, as well as to the police officer if a deaf person intends to lipread.

Interpreting techniques

At a police interview, an interpreter for a non-English speaker uses consecutive interpretation only (see p18), which is provided after the speaker (ie the police officer or non-English speaker) has stopped speaking. Sign-language interpreters speak at the same time as the deaf person signs. This is called 'voicing-over'.

Speaking styles

Speaking styles can influence the quality of interpreting. Below are some points to bear in mind:

- use straightforward, simple language
- use direct speech ('did you', not 'ask him if', 'did he')
- speak and refer to the deaf person or the non-English speaker directly
- avoid overlapping speech (especially in tape-recorded interviews)
- do not ask the interpreter questions or make inappropriate comments to the interpreter. Remember that the interpreter is there to repeat everything that is said.

Awareness of communication issues

The officer must constantly monitor the effectiveness of communication all through the interview. During questioning it may become clear that despite earlier assumptions, an interpreter is required after all.

Visual communication

Non-English speakers naturally tend to look at and respond to the person facilitating communication with them – the interpreter. They can be reminded at the beginning of the interview that the interpreter is not the person responsible for asking the questions, and that they should look at the officer. Naturally, a deaf person must look at a sign-language interpreter or lipspeaker all the time, and will not be able to look at the police officer. It is important when this happens that the officer remembers to look directly at the deaf person even though he or she will not always be able to look back. For a deaf person, taking part in an interview through an interpreter can be tiring. Whereas hearing people can rest their eyes and still hear what is being said, if a deaf person stops watching an interpreter information vital to communication may be missed. This means that for deaf people, breaks in interviews are particularly significant.

Non-verbal behaviour

Throughout the interview, the police officer should bear in mind non-verbal aspects of communication, such as:

- body language – correctly understanding the signals
- why the suspect may not be looking at the officer (see *Visual communication* above).

An interpreter who hears a police officer identifying non-verbal behaviour incorrectly faces a dilemma, particularly if there is no solicitor present to monitor such observations. The question as to how such matters are to be dealt with should be clarified at the pre-interview stage (see p30).

Working conditions for interpreters

The following items should be borne in mind:

- water
- provision or availability of refreshments in long interviews or if required to wait
- paper and pen or pencil in order to be able to make notes
- somewhere to put dictionaries, glossaries, etc
- breaks in long interviews – the quality of interpreting drops over time.

Interpreters should be allowed to indicate to the officer the need for a break when they sense that their interpreting may suffer because they are getting tired. There is obviously a need to stop *before* mistakes are made. Ideally, a short break should be taken every 20 to 30 minutes.

LEGAL ADVICE

Anyone who is arrested has the right to consult privately with a solicitor (see Code C, para 13.9 and *Conferences between solicitor and client,* p34). A police officer is not *necessarily* prohibited from interpreting at an interview of a detained person, although the practice is undesirable for reasons of impartiality. However, when an interpreter is needed in order for the suspect to obtain legal advice, a police officer is *not* allowed to act as interpreter. What the interpreter hears is covered by the same privilege that attaches to solicitor-client communications (p34). The solicitor, client and interpreter should agree on how interpreting is to be carried out:

- if the interpreter has the skills, a whispered version of what the suspect says may be provided simultaneously to the lawyer. This avoids the need to interrupt the non-English speaker and will shorten the conference.
- it is probably better to use consecutive interpreting for the lawyer's questions. If the solicitor gives lengthy explanations, the interpreter might prefer to whisper a version to the non-English speaker.

The interpreter may encounter dilemmas, particularly ones relating to cultural issues of which a lawyer may appear to be unaware. Examples would include accepted ways of remembering or noting the dates of significant events, whether within a particular year or a lifetime, procedures for proving dates of birth, naming conventions, gender-bound roles and so on.

WRITTEN VERSIONS

At interviews

Before the days of tape-recorded interviews, the interpreter had to write down verbatim all non-English questions and answers (*R v Attard* (1958), and see Home Office Circular 31/1964). This is still the situation if the interview is for some reason not tape-recorded, but increasing use of electronics has made it very rare for interpreters to have to produce a written version. 'There is no requirement for the interpreter to make a separate written note of the interview, unless the suspect is deaf or there is doubt about his hearing ability, in which case a contemporaneous note of the interview will be made by the officer . . . in addition to the tape-recording' (*Metropolitan Police Handbook for Interpreters,* IV.3). If the suspect elects to make a written statement under caution, the interpreter might be asked to assist by writing down *exactly* what is said in the foreign language and at the end will prepare an English translation. The interpreter should take care to stop at suitable intervals to give the officer an

46

oral translation so that, if necessary, questions may be asked to clarify the statement.

Transcripts

The transcribing of a video-taped interview is dealt with below (pp53-54). In the case of audio-recordings of interviews with non-English speakers, the same procedure should be followed as for video-recordings, with appropriate adaptations. Best practice is a double-column transcript, containing material in English in one column, and in the second language in the other. If this is not practicable for technical reasons (such as software or other practical aspects), each page of the separate English and second-language transcripts should cover the same number of minutes/amount of time in the interview. Transcribing recordings is time-consuming and should be done by someone with appropriate skills, who has the right languages, training and equipment, on the basis of clearly defined guidelines including, for example:

- guidance on how to identify significant non-verbal behaviour
- precise indications about how significant non-verbal material is to be recorded by transcribers
- what to do about overlapping material
- how to insert indications about time in the transcript
- what to do about material which cannot be heard or understood properly.

Guidance on making transcripts of police tape recordings was provided by the Court of Appeal in *R v Rampling* (1987).

PART III: WITNESSES AND VICTIMS

At the investigative stage witnesses to, and victims of, alleged crimes might be interviewed in any number of venues such as at the roadside, in a private house, or in hospital. There is no specific requirement for such interviews to be tape-recorded (other than in relation to *Child Witnesses*: see pp50-52). Police officers can exercise discretion about whether or not to record the interview, and written witness statements may be taken at a later date in a police station.

An interpreter should not be left alone with either victims or witnesses. If an appointment is made with an interpreter to visit the home of a witness or victim, the interpreter must always be accompanied by a police officer.

There are two standard techniques for police interviews. These are the 'cognitive' approach and 'management of conversation'. Both seek to create an environment in which the witness is able to relax sufficiently to be able to recall events in detail. An interpreter must exercise great skill to facilitate this.

Cognitive approach
The cognitive approach allows the interviewee to mentally re-live and recount events in a free-flowing way, with little interference from the interviewer. This technique allows the interviewee to control the flow of information whilst the interviewer listens (and takes notes). It is vital for the interpreter to hear the witness clearly, and for the police officer to hear the interpreter clearly. Unless technical facilities are available (as detailed under *Child witnesses*, pp54-56), the interpreter will have to sit near – possibly just behind and to one side of – the police officer and whisper softly into the officer's ear what the witness is saying. The technique involves the rendering being provided simultaneously (ie *chuchotage*: see p19). If the witness is speaking very quietly, the fact that the interpreter has to speak to the officer at the same time can make it difficult to hear the witness clearly enough to be accurate and not guess what the witness is saying.

Management of conversation
Conversation management involves a more structured approach, although this too will involve an open question at the beginning of the interview to establish detailed information. Open and specific questions are used to obtain information and interpreters must take great care to reflect the style of questioning used.

Written witness statements
Points raised in *R v Turnbull* (1976) should be observed by police officers when obtaining information from eye-witnesses or victims. Each of the following should be included in written statements of witnesses or victims:

> Amount of time under observation
> Distance
> Visibility
> Obstructions
> Known or seen before
> Any reason to remember
> Time lapse
> Error or material discrepancy.

Interpreters at police interviews, when a statement is being taken from a witness or victim, will be required to tell the witness in his or her own language what the English-language declaration on the witness statement (form MG14) says and to write out a translation underneath in the target language. The statement will be signed by the person making the statement and the signature witnessed – probably by the interpreter. The declaration reads:

48

This statement consisting of . . . pages each signed by me is true to the best of my knowledge and belief and I make it knowing that if it is tendered in evidence I shall be liable to prosecution if I have wilfully stated in it anything which I know to be false or do not believe to be true.

When a witness statement is written in a foreign language, the interpreter subsequently translates the statement into English (on a fresh form MG 14) and this translation may be used as an exhibit at court. It must therefore be identified by an exhibit label, completed and signed by the interpreter. The interpreter then makes a statement on a different form (MG 11) formally identifying the translation:

On (date) I attended at (police station) at the request of the police. There I recorded a statement in (language) at the dictation of (name) . . . I subsequently translated that statement into English and I produce the translation as exhibit (number). I am an official interpreter of the (police force) and I interpreted the above matters to the best of my skill and ability.

The procedures (which make the interpreter a potential witness) are thus:

(i) Foreign-language witness statement (on MG 14). This is referred to as 'the original statement' and is *not* produced as an exhibit in court. It is usually written down by the interpreter in the foreign language, as dictated by the witness.

(ii) English translation (on MG 14). Identified by the interpreter as an exhibit.

(iii) Interpreter's witness statement (MG 11). This explains the role of the interpreter and identifies the English translation.

Identification

Identification procedures are dealt with in PACE Code D. There are several possible methods when identification is in dispute:

• identification parade
• group identification
• video identification
• confrontation
• photograph identification.

An identification officer is appointed to organize and conduct these procedures. The interpreter's role is to assist the officer by explaining to the non-English speaking suspect what is happening, or is going to happen, or to interpret for a witness who is trying to make an identification.

49

CHILD WITNESSES

Criminal Justice Acts of 1988 and 1991 introduced fresh ways for children to give evidence in court in cases of violence or sexual abuse. Section 32A of the 1988 Act allows video-recorded interviews with children to be admitted in evidence in a criminal trial. Such a recording can spare a child from giving evidence in person and, if handled properly, is in the interests of the child and the interests of justice. This legislation demands a high level of inter-agency partnership, the two main players being local authority social services and the police. Co-operation between these two organizations and, for example, education authorities, the probation service and the medical profession in the area of child protection had been evolving since the 1970s, but the *Report of the Inquiry into Child Abuse* by Lady Justice Butler-Sloss (HMSO, 1987) gave an additional sense of urgency to the need for renewed standards of approach. A current explanation is provided in *Working Together* (Home Office and Department of Health, HMSO, 1988, revised 1991), and in the *Memorandum of Good Practice on video-recorded interviews with child witnesses for criminal proceedings* (Home Office and Department of Health, HMSO, 1992). The Memorandum draws upon the recommendations of the Home Office Advisory Group on Video Evidence and is based on advice within government departments and from professionals with practical experience of the investigation of child abuse. The publicity which attached to the Cleveland inquiry and other high-profile cases focused attention on the additional stress placed on children required to give evidence in court on matters of sexual abuse. The trauma for a child, particularly when a family member is accused of a criminal offence, can be immense. The courtroom environment is often oppressive. Recording the child's evidence on video can reduce stress. It also has the advantage that it occurs at an early stage. *Working Together* emphasises the need to involve children and families throughout the process of child protection investigations and states that:

> If a child or parent has communication difficulties, arrangements must be made to help them during interviews, and in the case of children or parents whose first language is not English, efforts should be made to help them have a clear understanding of what is happening and what may happen in the future. Enlisting the services of an interpreter should be considered, but care [must] be taken in their choice.

The *Memorandum of Good Practice* states:

> The joint investigating team should also consider whether there are any special factors arising from the child's cultural or religious background

which are relevant to planning an effective interview. In some cases it will be necessary for the team to seek advice in advance about particular ethnic customs and beliefs. Consideration of race, language, and also gender may influence the choice of interviewer. A child should be interviewed in his or her first language except in the most exceptional circumstances. (para 29)

It also makes reference to disabilities:

If the child has any disabilities, for example a speech or hearing impediment, or learning difficulties, particular care should be taken to develop effective strategies for the interview to minimise the effect of such disabilities . . . In some cases it may be necessary to pass through an appropriately skilled third party, for example a person who can use sign language. In others it might be necessary to consider asking such people to conduct the interview (see paragraph 2.24 . . .). As when any other language is used, a translation will need to be made available to the court. (para 2.10)

Planning a child interview

Information leading to an investigation of violence against, or sexual abuse of, a child might involve social work or other agencies who deal with family/child care cases. Alternatively, information may come to the police through a complaint from a member of the family, or from the public. Once it becomes apparent that a criminal offence may have been committed, an interview should be arranged as soon as practicable. The agency at the point of referral will contact the other agency and planning for the interview will begin. Planning is essential and requires input from each of the disciplines represented on the joint investigating team. If the matter is serious, this strategy meeting will include a senior police officer and a team leader from social services.

The interpreter

Even if the need for an interpreter is not raised at a first meeting, it will certainly be an item for consideration at a subsequent planning meeting for the video interview. Information about the child will be shared between team members and will include the need to use an interpreter. In some instances a separate meeting will be held with the interpreter to discuss the interview and clarify points arising from the *Memorandum of Good Practice*. The qualities required from an interpreter in this type of assignment are extensive. He or she should not only have excellent interpreting skills and a knowledge of the procedures, but should also:

. . . have empathy, be understanding and caring, patient, and have a sound knowledge of child development. . . . Children suddenly stop; they don't

51

want to talk about it any more. It takes absolutely ages. If they don't like
the interpreter you've had it and if the interpreter isn't very careful, the
children will 'shut up'. If [the interpreter] doesn't know about children -
forget it. (Police inspector)

Training

Recommendations in the *Report of the Inquiry into Child Abuse* (see above)
that all interviews should only be undertaken by people with training,
experience and an aptitude for talking with children are endorsed in the
Memorandum of Good Practice. The training undertaken by members of joint
investigative teams aims to raise their awareness and understanding of the basic
rules of evidence in criminal cases; they are not expected to adopt the style of
the professional advocate, but have to recognise and take proper account of the
rules and the law in interviewing children. This in turn suggests that
interpreters too should be provided with relevant training. At present, the
situation in many regions is that team members (social services and the police)
consider that specialised training is essential for interpreters who undertake this
work, but so far there is little relevant training available. It seems to be
generally recognised by practitioners that there should be rigorous selection and
monitoring procedures to identify appropriate interpreters for this work and that
training courses should be made available.

Video interviews

Ideally video interviews are conducted on appropriately equipped premises and
these are available in many areas, eg in hospitals, family centres or other
premises which have been adapted for the purpose. Purpose-built interview
rooms usually have two cameras: one to focus on the child and the other to take
in the whole room. Seating for the child, the interviewer and interpreter will be
placed appropriately. Other people, such as a parent or other appropriate adult
who has accompanied the child to the interview, will be encouraged to retire to
an observation room where they will be able to see and hear the interview, but
not be seen by the child. In some instances the interpreter will be required not
for the child, who speaks English, but for the adult who does not, when the
assignment will be carried out in simultaneous mode (pp18-19).

Language aspects of interviewing child witnesses on video

Many of the points addressed in this section apply also to standard interpreting
situations. However, because a video-taped interview with a child witness may
be used in substitution for the child's evidence-in-chief, it is critically important
to pay careful attention to every aspect of the interpreting process.

Interviewing a child witness without an interpreter

It is always preferable to interview a non-English speaking child in his or her own language rather than through an interpreter. Children who speak English as a second language should only be interviewed in English in the most exceptional circumstances (*Memorandum of Good Practice*, para 2.9). Qualified English-speaking interviewers who have some fluency in a second language should be sure that their language skills really are sufficient for proper interviewing of the particular child. Even if it is possible to interview a non-English speaking child in his or her own language, without an interpreter, certain language-related implications still remain and must be dealt with.

The video-recording of the interview will be entirely in a language other than English. A translation will have to be made available, both in order for its content to be assessed, and to the court (*Memorandum of Good Practice*, para 2.10). To do this, guidelines on transcription should be drawn up. It bears repeating that the following should be covered:

- guidance for transcribers on how to identify significant non-verbal behaviour
- precise indications about how such significant non-verbal material is to be recorded by transcribers
- what to do about overlapping material
- how to insert indications about time in the transcript
- what to do about material which cannot be heard or understood properly.

The three stages in transcribing and translating are:

- inserting a timing strip in the video-recording (if not already included)
- producing a complete original-language transcript of the interview
- translating the transcript of the interview.

Transcribing must be done by a competent person, following the guidelines above. Serious consideration should be given to the facilities made available to the transcriber. These may include video-play devices, headset, transcribing equipment (preferably with foot-control rewind), and word-processing means. On completion, it is advisable for the transcript to be checked against the original material by someone other than the transcriber. A competent person (who may be someone other than the transcriber) should then prepare an English translation of the source-language transcript of the interview. If he or she wishes, the translator should be able to view the video-recording before or while producing the translation. The original timings should be inserted as closely as possible in the English-language version. A final quality check of the translation against the original transcript should be made by somebody other

53

than the translator, to make sure that the English version is complete and accurate. Any remaining problems (items that were faint, inaudible or unclear in the original, or that cannot readily be put into English) should be referred to in accompanying notes.

Interviewing a child witness through an interpreter
Where a child witness is interviewed through an interpreter, the following points must be considered:

- interpreting what the child says
- interpreting what the interviewer says
- interpreting techniques
- use of equipment
- number of interpreters
- recording source language and interpreted material (video and audio)
- transcribing the interview
- translating the interview.

Interpreting techniques in respect of children
For non-English speakers, two main options are available: consecutive and simultaneous (pp18-19).

Consecutive interpreting
If consecutive interpreting of a child is chosen, the interpreter will need outstanding note-taking and short-term memory skills. The child must not be interrupted by the interpreter. Aspects such as hesitation and repetition may be relevant and the interpreter should try to reproduce these, but note-taking techniques do not normally allow for this. Even with high-calibre consecutive interpreting, the interview will be affected by the use of this technique. The interpreter gives an English version after the child stops speaking. The child may, however, begin to speak again before the interpreter has given the whole of the English rendering. It is then necessary to take further notes before the previous passage has been put into English for the interviewer.

Simultaneous interpreting
If simultaneous interpreting is chosen, the above problems are avoided. The options are 'whispered simultaneous' and 'electronic simultaneous' (pp18-19). In whispered simultaneous interpreting, the interpreter will sit close to the interviewer and literally whisper an English version of what the child is saying. The advantage is that a single interpreter can be used to relay both what the child says and what the interviewer says. However, this method also has a number of disadvantages when applied to children:

- the child may be distracted or upset by seeing and hearing somebody talking to the interviewer at the same time as he or she is speaking
- the interpreter will be less likely to hear the child clearly, and consequently may not interpret accurately
- the interviewer may not be able to hear the interpreter properly
- the interpreter's voice may be audible on the tape-recording of the interview, interfering with the recording of the child's voice
- it is not possible to record the English version whispered by the interpreter. In order to obtain a written English version of what the child has said, it will be necessary to first transcribe everything said by the child and then translate it into English
- if a single interpreter is used throughout a lengthy interview, fatigue may lead to mistakes being made.

Combined system

As outlined, there are considerable disadvantages in using either consecutive interpreting or whispered simultaneous interpreting with children. Most of these disadvantages can be avoided by a combined system. In this, the consecutive mode is retained for what the interviewer says to the child. The interviewer then follows what the child says through a simultaneous version provided from a separate observation room and transmitted electronically. Where an observation room exists, the necessary facilities for providing sound in it will already exist. Other technical aspects need to be dealt with, ie conveying the interpreter's voice to the ear of the interviewer so that the interviewer can follow and respond to what the child is saying; recording the interpreter's voice; good-quality sound to the interpreter, preferably provided through earphones, with the interpreter being able to control the volume; a high-fidelity microphone should be used (unclear sound increases the stress on interpreters and impairs the quality of performance); there should be no extraneous noise in the observation room; all practicable measures must be taken to provide the best possible sound quality for interpreters, transcribers and listeners (immediate and later).

Interpreting the interviewer's remarks to the child

Everything that the interviewer says to the child has to be put into the child's language. This will have to be done in the consecutive mode, ie after the interviewer has finished speaking. The consecutive interpreter will be in the interview room. Thought should be given to where that interpreter is going to sit and what to tell the child about this third person. The interpreter may or may not need to take notes.

Breaks

If the interview is a long one, at some stage the simultaneous interpreter in the observation room will become tired. This can have adverse effects on concentration and, consequently, on performance. The significance and sensitive nature of the interview make it vital for the interpreter to be as accurate as is humanly possible. It is therefore highly desirable for two interpreters to take it in turns to interpret in the observation room. If this is not possible, the interpreter should have short breaks as appropriate. Normally simultaneous interpreters try to avoid spells of longer than 30 minutes.

The English version of an interpreted interview

After the interview, a decision will need to be taken about first transcribing and then translating what the child said. One alternative is to follow the full procedure for transcribing and translating non-English material as detailed above in the section on *Interviewing a child witness without an interpreter* (p53). The alternative is to transcribe only the interpreter's English version, where this has been clearly recorded. Any such decision must take into account the fact that because of time constraints, even the best interpreter can make mistakes. If only the interpreted English version is transcribed, and not the child's original words, when the draft transcript has been produced a linguistically competent person (preferably a mother-tongue speaker of the child's language) should watch the video-recording and check the interpreter's rendering against what the child said. The English-language transcript can then be corrected for interpreter errors.

When transcribing and, as appropriate, translating the interview, the procedure and points made in *Interviewing a child witness without an interpreter* should be borne in mind.

Status and quality of interpreted evidence

It is important to bear in mind that neither a written transcript nor the English-language version of what the child said is original evidence. The English-language translation is simply the best evidence readily available to English speakers. However, in a transcript it is not possible to indicate accurately, completely or properly a variety of material about body language, direction of gaze, stress, tone of voice, and so on. The video-recording should therefore be viewed both in the evaluation phase and during any subsequent use in court, accompanied either by the written English transcript or, where available, the recording of the interpreter's electronic simultaneous version. In addition, when an English speaker views the video-recording, possible differences in cultural conventions and patterns should be considered. It may be necessary to seek competent advice in connection with such matters, not only before the interview (*Memorandum of Good Practice,* para 2.9), but afterwards.

If the interpreters are sensitive, experienced and skilled in both simultaneous and consecutive interpreting, and provided that the technical arrangements are made properly, then the combined use of two interpreting techniques should work well for accurately conveying to the interviewer what the child says to the interviewer and enabling the interviewer to communicate effectively with the child.

Although the ideal procedure outlined above sounds complex, the technical equipment needed for it is readily available. With appropriate interpreters, it should make it possible to achieve proper communication. It is important to realise that a particularly high level of skill is required to accurately and fully interpret what the child says by means of the consecutive technique. In addition, the dynamics of the interview are likely to be adversely affected by the interruptions in child-interviewer communication that result from using this technique.

Interpreting for a non-English speaking parent
When a non-English speaking parent of a child witness follows the interview from the observation room, the interpreter can use the whispered simultaneous technique. A microphone, portable amplification equipment and headphones (wired or wireless system) for both interpreter and listener can reduce physical and other stress by improving acoustics and reducing the need for physical proximity.

Interpreting for deaf and hearing-impaired child witnesses
In the case of deaf and hearing-impaired child witnesses, consideration should be given to providing the following:

- appropriate interpreters for children fluent in British Sign Language (BSL) or another sign language (Sign-Supported English, Paget-Gorman etc)
- induction loop for children with hearing aids
- other technical aids to communication.

Interviewing a deaf child through an interpreter
When the child signs, the interpreter who conveys what the child says to the interviewer will need to see the child properly and must therefore be present in the interview room. The interpreter will use the simultaneous technique ('voicing-over': pp20, 44). Similarly, he or she will also convey what the interviewer says to the child by signing simultaneously. Measures must be taken to ensure that the interpreter's voice is *clearly* recorded so that it can later be readily transcribed. Without proper transcription, it will be difficult to make effective use of what the child said. Unless more than one interpreter is employed, consideration should be given to providing breaks for the interpreter.

Interviewing a deaf child without an interpreter

If the interviewer is a competent signer and good communication can be achieved directly between interviewer and child, the interview may be conducted on video without an interpreter. So that the interview can later be accurately translated into English, great care must be taken to ensure that the signing frames (including the hands, faces and body down to just below the waist) of both parties – child and interviewer – are clearly visible on camera. Quality control of the translation process (BSL or similar to written English) should be carried out. Guidelines should be drawn up to assist translators.

Interpreting for a deaf or hearing-impaired parent

A deaf or hearing-impaired parent of a hearing child may follow the interview from inside the interview room or from a separate observation room. This will make it necessary to ensure that the appropriate facilities are provided (interpreting into the correct variety of sign language; other human or technical aids to communication).

Providing an interpreter to work into (or from) a sign language other than BSL is likely to be difficult to arrange and ample time should be provided for locating a suitable person (see the communication methods given on p20 in Chapter 1). Interpreters fluent in Irish Sign Language and American Sign Language (ASL) are likely to be more readily available in Britain than those in other sign languages.

CHAPTER 3

Entry to the United Kingdom

Language issues are particularly important at all stages of Customs and Excise and immigration procedures. Many people who are affected by such procedures do not speak fluent English, and may also not be literate in that language. In addition, interviews may be carried out when people are least able to cope with questioning in a foreign language, having just had a long and tiring journey, possibly coming at the end of an extended period of private suffering. In this respect, all of the comments in the last chapter about assessing language ability and related matters apply equally to this chapter. An additional factor is that asylum seekers who have been tortured (see pp61-62) may not be able to talk easily, quickly or fluently about the circumstances. Nor will they necessarily trust people or be able to complete questionnaires promptly.

PART I: ENTRY PROCEDURES

People seeking entry into the United Kingdom may fall into one or more categories: short-stay visitors such as those on holiday or business; students; employees with work permits; people seeking residence on a long-term basis such as marriage to a British citizen or because they are fleeing from persecution in their country of origin.

Entry and asylum
Entry is subject to the Immigration Acts 1971 and 1988 and the Asylum and Immigration Appeals Act 1993. These control entry to the country and the rights to remain of people already in the UK (including the Common Travel Area of the European Union). Immigration Rules are made by the Secretary of State for the Home Department under relevant Acts of Parliament (the present Rules have been in force since 1994). People subject to immigration control may not enter or remain in the UK except with leave. This may be granted to last indefinitely or for a limited period. If the latter, an immigrant is subject to further conditions, eg restricting employment.

Travel documentation, eg passport and visa applications (for people from countries on a specified list who may not travel to the UK without a visa or who are seeking entry in a specific visa-requiring category), is generally handled in a person's own country. Applications are checked by entrance clearance officers. The regulations abroad are administered by officials of the Foreign and

Commonwealth Office. These procedures are known as 'before-entry control' and are carried out in British embassies, high commissions or consulates.

Other procedures may include applications for asylum or visitor applications from non-visa countries at a port of entry. These are dealt with by officers of the Immigration Service. Immigration officers have the power to grant or refuse entry, to detain people, to search individuals and their luggage, to read papers and letters, and to require people to undergo a medical examination.

If applications are made by individuals for variations to the original documentation after they have entered the UK, these are dealt with under procedures known as 'after-entry control'. They may include applications for a change in, or extension to, a visa; to regularise an illegal immigrant's situation; or to seek asylum because circumstances in the country of origin have changed. The circumstances and conditions for issue of such visa variations are restrictive. Once an application is made for asylum, the Home Office becomes responsible for administering the application. Information to respond to such an application may be elicited by questionnaire, interview or at a personal hearing.

The full definition of a refugee is contained in Article 1 of the 1951 United Nations Convention Relating to the Status of Refugees as amended by the 1967 Protocol ('the Convention'). The UK is a signatory to the Convention and Protocol and has ratified both. The Immigration Acts 1971 and 1988 do not mention the Convention, but asylum matters are covered in the Asylum and Immigration Appeals Act 1993, which states in section 1 that asylum applications are defined in the terms of the Convention, and in section 2 that 'nothing in the immigration rules shall lay down any practice which would be contrary to the Convention'. The Immigration Rules confirm that applications will be decided in accordance with UN obligations (see para 328).

Immigration and asylum procedures may include one or more of the following stages:

- visa application abroad (comprising form-filling and interview)
- port applications (*pro forma* interview at port, questionnaire)
- final declaration at the end of an interview: the officer reads this out, asking the applicant whether he or she has been happy with the interview, has understood everything and has said all that he or she wishes to say
- self-completion questionnaire (usually four weeks to respond)
- another interview with an immigration officer for 'further questions'
- illegal entry interview
- asylum interview (where officials try to obtain information to be used in a decision on whether to grant asylum)
- final refusal interview

- appeal in Britain on behalf of an applicant abroad who has been refused entry and sent away or refused entry clearance
- appeal in Britain by an applicant who is already in the country (including 'overstayers' of earlier leave to enter)
- applications to the Immigration Appellate Authority (IAA: see pp64-66).

Engaging an interpreter

As in all other legal processes, an interpreter engaged for immigration interviews or similar procedures, including appeal tribunals, must have high-level skills in English and the other language, be an experienced and competent interpreter, and be familiar with the procedures for which interpreting is needed.

Impartiality is an important requirement of interpreters across the legal system, as shown by corresponding references in interpreter codes of ethics. Bias on the part of interpreters for immigration (especially asylum) interviews and hearings can be particularly harmful, and people who engage such interpreters should bear this in mind.

People who need to use the services of interpreters include immigration officers at ports of entry; the Home Office (Immigration Service Ports Directorate); the Immigration Appellate Authority; immigration lawyers; specialist advisory organizations; the police in any initial interviewing of illegal immigrants; and the immigration authorities when interviewing alleged illegal entrants.

Asylum

Asylum interviews tend to have a minimum of two stages. The first of these is the *pro forma* stage, where brief initial details are taken and the fact that the person wants to make an asylum claim is asserted. It is rare for legal representatives to be present, or indeed to be allowed to be present, at this stage. At the second interview permission is granted for a legal representative, and for that representative's interpreter, to attend, but this is a concession only. It is made quite clear that the representatives are there as 'observers only'. Lawyers and other people who specialise in immigration matters report that this can lead to problems where the conduct of the interview or the standard of interpreting is challenged.

The [official] interpreter kept asking me for simple words. This was in breach of the regulations because the official interpreter is not supposed to have any contact with us. (Independent interpreter)

The [Home Office] interpreter was using the familiar form of address to the person being interviewed. This was bad etiquette and offensive to the person. It puts the interviewee at a disadvantage and this sort of thing happens far too often. (Independent interpreter)

Organizations such as the Refugee Legal Centre, the Joint Council for the Welfare of Immigrants and the Medical Foundation for the Care of Victims of Torture all employ interpreters to assist in communicating at interviews. Asylum seekers who have experienced torture are likely to arrive at ports of entry to the UK in a traumatised state and to be unable to cope effectively with the questions they are confronted with. Organizations dealing with torture victims know that it can take a long time to build sufficient trust to talk freely about such experiences. Interpreters engaged by such organizations, particularly those which prepare medico-legal reports, are particularly aware of the sensitive nature of their work. It can be difficult to persuade a torture victim that the interpreter is impartial and will treat what is said with the utmost confidentiality. Reports for asylum applications may require medical and/or psychiatric examinations. In this area of work the skill of the interpreter and the working relationship with the medical practitioner are extremely important. Induction courses and training programmes for interpreters serve to raise standards and to provide opportunities for an exchange of useful information. Organizations like the Medical Foundation for the Care of Victims of Torture provide a support system for their interpreters and also demonstrate an active concern for interpreting standards – seemingly in marked contrast to some official bodies.

Dealing with harrowing information

When the 'case history' of an asylum seeker who has been tortured is being elicited, the interpreter may find it harrowing to have to listen to and relay details of suffering and atrocities. Non-English speakers are likely to be distressed, and consequently may express themselves incoherently or unclearly. There is always a risk that these factors will have an adverse effect on the highly accurate interpreting that is so absolutely necessary in this context. Failure by an interpreter to accurately convey in English 'I looked round to see my mother-in-law being spattered with bullets', may make the difference between the success or failure of an asylum seeker's application.

Pre-interview briefing

The interpreter should try to be aware of the political background to a specific asylum claim. It is essential that the interpreter is not, or is not perceived to be, from an opposite party or sympathetic to the regime of the alleged torturing state. A pre-interview briefing with a lawyer or adviser who has knowledge of the situation in the country in question can be helpful. Specialists include the Refugee Legal Centre, the Immigration Advisory Service and lawyers from the Immigration Law Practitioners Association (ILPA). Whilst most people who work for the Legal Centre and the Advisory Service are not lawyers, they will have been specifically trained by the organization in question to advise and represent potential immigrants or asylum seekers.

Record of interview

Except where an immigrant is being interviewed in a situation covered by the Police and Criminal Evidence Act 1984 (PACE) (see p66 and, generally, Chapter 2), no regular provision is made at any of the immigration procedure stages for an electronic recording of what is said. Applicants who wish to challenge the accuracy of interpreting at any stage in the procedure therefore have no way of proving that errors have occurred. The ILPA did make a request for full tape-recording facilities to be installed when new interviewing facilities were being installed, but this has not yet resulted in such arrangements. Consequently, it is particularly difficult to mount challenges to interpreting during immigration procedures. In cases where appeals are brought on the ground that a particular interpreter at some stage in an application has acted incompetently or in a biased fashion, affidavits are usually submitted by the interpreter in question to the effect that he or she interpreted very carefully and accurately, in addition to having many years of experience and impressive qualifications (for an example of such an appeal, see *R v Secretary of State for the Home Department, ex parte Wu* (1991)). In the light of such submissions and the applicant's total inability to submit evidence of what was said in the foreign language as compared with what was noted in English, appeals brought on the grounds of an interpreter's poor or biased performance are rarely successful.

> Time and again inappropriate interpreters are used by the authorities. There is a lack of care regarding compatibility of language and quality control. Interpreters who have been challenged and who are known by the authorities to be incompetent continue to be engaged at these interviews and appeals. (Solicitor)

> Officials seem to think, for example, that anyone from North Africa and Turkey can interpret for an Algerian; there is a disregard for the differences in language and dialect and for the problems of communication which can then arise. There is frequent, and inappropriate use of Portuguese speakers to interpret for Algerians. (Solicitor)

An illustration of the difficulties that an interpreter's performance may cause to someone applying for permission to enter Britain is provided by *In re H K* (1967), in which the official Immigration Department interpreter was unable to provide a translation of a Pakistani Urdu-language school-leaving certificate. In the absence of any other document establishing the applicant's age – the key factor for a decision about his right to enter the United Kingdom as the child of a Commonwealth citizen ordinarily resident in the United Kingdom – that certificate was critical. As was pointed out on appeal, the interpreter's inability to decipher the Urdu document deprived the boy of a fair opportunity to present his case, and he was detained

The upshot in *In re H K* was that crucial evidence that would have been readily available if the document had been in a language which the official himself could read, was simply ignored. Again, as the appellate court commented, the manner in which the immigration officer treated the school-leaving certificate was to merely look at it '. . . as a paper in a foreign language. His interpreter could not read it adequately, and the immigration officer took a peremptory view of the document . . .'. In that case as elsewhere in the immigration system, the officer, '. . . having judicial power curtailing the right of a Commonwealth subject, had, in a sense, to be an investigating officer and give a decision as well'. This episode highlights the often crucial importance of interpreters being literate in *both* languages, something which appears to be regularly ignored.

Aware of difficulties that regularly occur with 'official' Immigration Service interpreters, legal representatives have been advised in the ILPA *Best Practice Guide* to take along their own independent interpreter when attending asylum interviews. The role of this additional interpreter is to identify instances of incorrect renderings and situations where the interpreter asks questions instead of the immigration officer, comments on answers given, or otherwise interferes in the interview. Such monitoring practices have developed in response to documented instances of official interpreters failing to meet proper standards.

Where an independent interpreter is present at an asylum (or other immigration) interview, it is standard practice for the immigration officer to begin by stipulating that any interpreting-related objections must be submitted *at the end* of the interview. This leads to the absurd situation whereby there may be sheets of objections which the officer will only consider at the conclusion of the interview, and yet the objections are of such a nature as to make the whole interview worthless. Because challenges to incorrect renderings are not allowed as the interview proceeds, the result is that incorrect, distorted or incomplete information may be provided throughout. In one interview the interpreter provided by the authorities could not translate very simple asylum-related words and phrases such as 'unions', 'fighting for the right to organize', or 'riots'. This official interpreter sought assistance from the independent interpreter. Ultimately, that interview was abandoned.

IMMIGRATION APPEALS

About 30,000 appeals against immigration decisions are made each year to the Immigration Appellate Authority (IAA). On average, 80 per cent of these require an interpreter. There are full-time IAA centres in Glasgow, Leeds, Manchester, Birmingham, Hatton Cross, Wood Green and Central London. Part-time centres are located in Belfast, Cardiff, Banbury and Gravesend. The law requires appeals to be completed within 42 days, which places pressure on the parties in the preparation of cases, particularly those involving a non-English speaker. The avenue of appeal is to an adjudicator, then to the Immigration Appeals Tribunal, and finally to the Court of Appeal on a point of law. Some deportation appeals leapfrog the adjudicator and go straight to the tribunal for a full hearing. Some asylum appellants will not, in future, be permitted to apply for leave to appeal to the tribunal.

Stage I: Adjudications

The adjudicator is a solicitor or barrister of at least seven years standing, some being practising lawyers, others having an academic background. The appeal represents a major stage in an application to enter or remain in Britain. If this is lost, it is possible to apply for leave to appeal to the Immigration Appeals Tribunal, and thereafter to apply for leave to appeal to the Court of Appeal.

In contrast to the situation of a non-English speaker facing criminal charges (see Chapters 2 and 4), the interpreter provided by the authorities does not give the immigration applicant a simultaneous rendering of *everything* said at the hearing. The interpreter renders only questions to the witness and his or her replies. If the appellant speaks no English, he or she is therefore unaware of much that is occurring (eg discussions about procedure or the weight to be given to evidence). If the appellant is not aware of what has been said, quite substantial miscarriages of justice can result. Thus the basic principle that has been applied to criminal cases tried by English courts ever since *R* v *Lee Kun* (1916) (see Chapter 4) – ie that even when a defendant who does not understand English is represented by a lawyer, the evidence must still be interpreted – does *not* apply to people asserting claims in immigration hearings.

Despite the need for high-quality interpreting at the adjudication stage (as elsewhere in the legal process), problems exist and instances have been documented, for example, of interpreters being engaged who do not speak the same dialect as the applicant.

Engaging interpreters for immigration appeals

In 1993, the IAA introduced *Guidance Notes and Instructions for Casually-Employed Interpreters*. These have been revised and are intended to serve interpreters in much the same way as interpreter notes of guidance produced by some police forces do: see Chapter 2. The notes reflect a view of interpreters as resources to be used to process appeals in the most cost-effective manner. Much of the material deals in detail with late arrival by interpreters, failure to appear and working hours. Brief instructions are given about conduct, interpreting methods and standards of performance. It is stipulated that interpreters are to interpret *'sentence by sentence'* (italics supplied), speaking slowly and clearly in order to enable the adjudicator to write everything down. This conveys the unfortunate impression that the authorities are having difficulties with their interpreters, who seem to make a habit of arriving late or failing to turn up for engagements, and whose professionalism is in doubt. The document gives no indication of criteria for admission to the panel of approved interpreters: it would appear that applicants simply have to list the languages they claim to speak, read and write. There is no reference to any attempt to screen interpreters on the grounds of political or other bias and the document is silent on the subject of interpreting skills and experience.

Stage II: The Immigration Appeals Tribunal

The Immigration Appeals Tribunal has a UK-wide jurisdiction and exists to hear appeals brought by the Home Office against decisions made at an earlier adjudication, or by an individual whose application to remain has been rejected. Representations are made by the Home Office presenting officer and by the lawyer on behalf of the appellant (if one has been appointed). The tribunal hears witnesses and asks questions of the appellant.

PART II: HER MAJESTY'S CUSTOMS AND EXCISE

Customs and Excise officers have the power to detain, investigate and prosecute people suspected of committing offences. They are responsible for law enforcement at ports, airports, rivers and tunnels and much of their work relates to drug trafficking, smuggling and associated items. Although customs officers are bound by the Police and Criminal Evidence Act 1984 (PACE) and the Codes of Practice pursuant to that Act, for the purposes of interviewing suspects, investigators' powers are wider than those given to the police. The Customs and Excise Management Act 1979 and delegated legislation allow officers to stop and search people and vehicles. The legislation also sets out the rules by which officers can question people, the quantity of goods which can be brought into the country and the relevant duties to be levied. Vehicles can be seized if, for example, they have been used to bring drugs into the UK.

Power to detain

Section 170(2) Customs and Excise Management Act 1979 provides:

Without prejudice to any other provision of the Customs and Excise Acts 1979, if any person is, in relation to any goods, in any way knowingly concerned in any fraudulent evasion or attempt at evasion–

(a) of any duty chargeable on the goods;

(b) of any prohibition or restriction for the time being in force with respect to the goods under or by virtue of any enactment; or

(c) of any provision of the Customs and Excise Acts 1979 applicable to the goods,

he shall be guilty of an offence under this section and may be arrested.

Customs officers and interpreter provision

Measures like the Misuse of Drugs Act 1971 give Customs and Excise officers the power to search people and vehicles and prevent the import or export of drugs or funds related to drug trafficking. Officers are graded according to the Civil Service hierarchy. A team of anti-smuggling officers may consist of a cross-section of grades, with a higher executive officer as team leader. The investigating officer, whatever his or her rank, is likely to be the officer who detected the offence and he or she will become the lead officer at interview. A designated officer will have the task of custody officer.

Many officers have language skills and they tend to be called to facilitate matters when someone detained for questioning appears to have difficulty communicating in English. However, when it has been established by the custody officer that a detainee needs an interpreter, it is usual practice for the investigation process to be held up until a proper interpreter arrives.

Interpreters are used on a regular basis at the major points of entry into the United Kingdom, and personnel in the Customs and Excise control room are generally responsible for carrying out procedures for contacting and appointing them. Interpreters may then be obtained by the same method for each subsequent court appearance (where they are required), rather than the court or the police taking responsibility for finding an interpreter for the proceedings.

Interview procedures

The procedures for interviewing people suspected of offences are governed by PACE and the Codes of Practice. The rights and entitlements of people detained by customs officers are as described in relation to police interviews of suspects in Chapter 2. The 'Notice to Detained Persons' and 'Notice of Entitlements' used by Customs and Excise, which have been translated into a number of languages, are similar to those produced by the Home Office for police officers.

The duty solicitor scheme extends to Customs and Excise investigations and facilities are made available for private consultations with a detainee. Interviews by customs officers are held in properly equipped rooms and tape-recorded pursuant to the PACE Codes of Practice: see again Chapter 2.

The physical and mental stress for an interpreter in Customs and Excise interviews can be just as great as in police interviews. There are no guidelines or specific training programmes for interpreters working with customs officers, and none for officers about how to work through an interpreter.

Even people with good conversational English don't know the word solicitor or even interpreter and it is a matter of pride on the part of many suspects to assume a knowledge of English. This is a big problem. (Interpreter)

It is the investigating officer's nightmare having to have an interpreter. (Customs officer)

Most of the interpreters are good, and a real plus is having one with a real knowledge of the suspect's language and culture. (Customs officer)

If someone is found carrying drugs at the time of arrest they will be handed a form which explains that unless an appeal is lodged, the bulk of the drugs will be destroyed. In addition, property and clothes may be taken from the suspect and a list of these items will then be made and handed to the person. When an arrest is made, it is possible that items of clothing and possessions will be confiscated because the customs officer will consider that they have come into contact with drugs. This may apply even to children's clothing and toys. Naturally, this can be traumatic for all concerned. When it happens to people who do not speak English, interpreters engaged for the assignment may find that they have to muster interpersonal skills which go beyond the narrower definition of an interpreter's role. Although a degree of sensitivity is desirable, interpreters can find this stressful when striving to maintain professional standards of responsibility and detachment (Chapter 7).

The customs officer will decide if there is sufficient evidence to charge the suspect with an offence and the relevant information is then presented to the designated custody officer. If the decision is to charge the detainee, formal procedures then take place at a police station because customs officers do *not* have specific statutory powers to act themselves. The interpreter employed at the Customs and Excise interview is then expected to attend at the relevant police station. This is one reason why assignments for HM Customs and Excise can be prolonged.

Customs interviews are very long, sometimes all day and all night; interpreters only get a rest when the tape needs changing. (Interpreter)

Summaries and transcripts
Summaries of taped interviews are prepared by case officers. Transcripts of taped interviews are prepared only if specifically requested by the defence lawyer or if the departmental solicitor deems it necessary. Although transcribing work, whether in English or a foreign language, may be sent out to private transcription agencies, the person who interpreted at the interview is still, on occasion, required to provide a bilingual transcript. It should be noted that

68

transcribing a taped interview can take many hours of intensive work, a point not always appreciated by defence or prosecution, particularly when the issue of payment arises. If the interpreter produces the transcript, then that interpreter cannot be engaged to interpret at the court as he or she might be called as a witness to the transcription.

Performance evaluation

Evaluation forms exist for officers to enter their observations about an interpreter's performance. The form asks for the officer's opinions on:

- interpreting standard (to include a possible assessment of whether the interpreter translates literally, or embellishes questions);
- availability (to include time taken to reach airport, own transport, etc);
- effectiveness as a court witness (to be completed as appropriate);
- any other observations, eg transcribing ability and time taken.

These are used by Customs and Excise coordinators of interpreting services to monitor interpreter provision and standards. As explained above (pp17 and 22), a requirement to be 'literal' does not guarantee accurate interpreting performance. 'Literal' renderings can themselves distort communication, and questions which are not interpreted 'word-for-word' are not necessarily 'embellished' because of an interpreter's misplaced sense of style, but rather worded carefully in such a way as to ask the question accurately. The reference under 'interpreting standard' in the Customs and Excise evaluation form to translating literally indicates a failure to understand these communication issues. As a result, evaluations carried out by officers who probably lack both professional interpreting expertise and specific linguistic skills are likely to be untrustworthy indicators of interpreter performance. Monitoring interpreters' performance is certainly a desirable state of affairs, but this is a complex matter which needs to be carried out by experts on the basis of objective criteria.

CHAPTER 4

Interpreters and the Courts

Today, the need for interpreters when non-English speakers and deaf people are involved in court proceedings (whether as defendants or witnesses) would appear to be self-evident, although over the centuries many such people have been tried in both English and other courts without the benefit of any language assistance, let alone impartial and competent interpreting.

A key aspect of all court-based interpreting situations is the working relationship which should be recognised as existing between interpreters, the judiciary (ie the judges or magistrates), lawyers, administrators and other practitioners. As things stand at the moment, there is nobody who can be said to have full and final responsibility for the performance and quality of interpreting in the court. Is it the magistrate, is it the judge, is it the lawyer, or is it actually the interpreter? Perhaps it is the person who engaged the interpreter? At the time of writing, even the responsibility for engaging an interpreter is in dispute, as reflected in reports and correspondence in the legal press (*New Law Journal*, 5/19 July 1996).

The quality of justice is enhanced if all concerned are prepared to act efficiently when an interpreting situation arises. In this connection also, although an interpreter who is not a lawyer cannot be expected to know all the relevant law, some degree of familiarity with 'legal thinking' is a considerable asset. One purpose of this chapter is to provide interpreters with some basic information about the operation of the court system in England and Wales.

Apart from legal concepts (the *what*), it is very helpful for interpreters to become less overwhelmed by legal *settings* (the *where*). Consequently, in addition to taking any suitable courses which are available, any would-be court interpreter should be sure to visit various court venues before accepting a first assignment. This will help familiarise them with such things as basic procedures, terminology and court layout. Telling a court usher (the *who*) about the purpose of a court visit is advisable and can generate considerable assistance.

For an interpreter, a court is a very different environment from that of an interview or meeting held out of public view. In court, the interpreter is – unnervingly – exposed to public scrutiny. In addition, he or she may have the feeling of not quite fitting in and being somewhat isolated: not a mere observer, but not a regular member of the 'court team' either. Courts are also busy, impersonal places, which can be disconcerting for anyone not used to them. Familiarity with the layout of court buildings and the people involved helps to build up confidence (see *Court personnel*, p73 below).

The interpreter should learn and rehearse the special language of the courts (in both languages) so that the right terms spring readily to mind when working in court. One technique – where possible – is to read reports of legal cases in *both* languages. It is also highly desirable to keep up-to-date with events in the other country. Here such things as satellite television, radio, newspapers, magazines, the Internet and its various discussion groups and forums can prove invaluable. They also help keep the interpreter acquainted with the latest developments in slang and other specialised areas of language.

Unlike many other countries, the United Kingdom has no codes of criminal or civil procedure. In the courts, interpreters will hear many legal and statutory references. For example, offences are dealt with under provisions such as the Offences Against the Person Act 1861, Theft Act 1968 (and 1972), Criminal Damage Act 1971, Road Traffic Acts and so on. References to Acts, Rules, Regulations and Practice Directions are so multifarious that even a lawyer cannot hope to keep them all in mind. Interpreters will, however, find it helpful to note their general structure and be precise in rendering the use of terms such as 'section', 'sub-section', 'paragraph' and 'sub-paragraph'. They may also find it helpful to acquire copies (perhaps second-hand) of the lawyers' 'Bible', such as *Archbold, Stone's Justices' Manual* and *County Court Practice,* in order to be able to make lists of terms they are likely to encounter in the relevant court setting.

PART I: COURTS IN ENGLAND AND WALES

This chapter focuses on interpreting in criminal proceedings. In principle, the same basic elements apply to the provision of interpretation in civil proceedings – with some modifications according to the exact subject matter or procedure. A major difference, however, is that in many civil proceedings, for example in the county courts, there is no strict legal authority which compels the provision of an interpreter by or with the funding of the authorities, even though certain civil cases may have criminal implications (*In the Estate of Fuld (1965)*) or natural justice might be infringed if there is no interpreting (*Kashich v Kashich (1951)*). Even if the court requires interpretation to be provided, it is currently unclear where the responsibility for payment in such cases lies. One aspect of the work of the civil courts forms part of Chapter 5, *Working with the Probation Service,* where the role of interpreters in relation to the Family Court Welfare Service is examined.

Magistrates' courts
The first tier of criminal courts in England and Wales is represented by the magistrates' courts. These are essentially local courts of summary jurisdiction dealing principally with matters arising in their own area, which is referred to as

a Petty Sessional Division (PSD). Many minor offences – known as 'summary offences' – can only be tried in the magistrates' court. Some 97 per cent of all criminal cases are dealt with in this way. Youth courts – comprised of specially trained magistrates – deal with the vast majority of criminal proceedings against people who are under 18 years old: see *Youth courts*, pp112-114.

Cases are usually dealt with by lay magistrates (called justices of the peace – 'JPs'). These are members of the local community, not qualified in law, who act on a voluntary basis and are advised by justices' clerks and other legal advisors or 'court clerks'. In many courts, the clerk sits in front of the magistrates, slightly below the bench, facing the body of the court.

Particularly in London and larger urban centres, cases may be dealt with by stipendiary magistrates. Stipendiaries are lawyers who are paid a 'stipend' (nowadays a regular salary) for discharging this full-time responsibility. The collective name for magistrates is 'a bench'. Usually three lay magistrates, one of whom acts as chairman, sit as a bench to hear cases. Stipendiary magistrates can, and usually do, sit on their own to hear cases.

Magistrates' powers are laid down by Act of Parliament. Thus an interpreter might expect to hear references, for example to the Magistrates' Courts Act 1980 (which governs many basic procedures), the Bail Act 1976, and in the Crown Court, various 'Criminal Justice Acts' which affect sentencing.

The Crown Court

The second tier of criminal courts is represented by the Crown Court. The Crown Court was created by the Courts Act 1971 and sits at some 90 Crown Court centres throughout England and Wales. Generally speaking, this court deals with more serious offences, such as murder, rape or robbery. But often the offence is less serious, such as shoplifting or a comparatively minor form of physical or sexual assault. People accused of certain criminal offences – known as 'either way' offences – have a right to elect trial by jury (see *Court Procedures* under the heading *Either way offences and mode of trial*, p106). If they do not, they are dealt with in the magistrates' court. The Crown Court has jurisdiction over all criminal offences triable 'on indictment', a term which includes not only those very serious cases which can only be tried in this way but also 'either way' offences already mentioned.

Judges of the Crown Court are all professional judges. In the main they are circuit judges (the regular judges of the court), recorders or assistant recorders (practising barristers or solicitors who sit part-time). A High Court judge will sit in the Crown Court to deal with the more serious cases.

Trials are held before a jury of twelve ordinary members of the public. Juries are chosen at random from the electoral roll. Both prosecution and defence can challenge particular jurors – for example, on the grounds that the juror is disqualified or ineligible, or is or might be partial or biased. There are also limited rights to ask jurors to stand down without giving a reason. Each member of the jury is required to swear an oath:

> I will faithfully try the several issues joined between our sovereign lady the Queen and the prisoner at the Bar, and give a true verdict according to the evidence.

The jury decides whether the accused is guilty or not guilty, by considering all the evidence in the case. Jury deliberations are confidential.

Unlike magistrates – the 'deciders of facts' in the magistrates' courts – jurors are not trained to focus on evidence or to discount subjective impressions. For example, they might be confused by the 'nodding-head syndrome' that occurs frequently in sign-language conversations. This feature indicates that the message is being *understood*, and not necessarily that it is being agreed with. Thus a sign-language witness may nod during cross-examination, but then the interpreter may render the response in English as 'No'. Unless the jurors are aware of the existence of the syndrome, they may wrongly conclude that either the witness is lying or the interpreter is incompetent. There is a responsibility on the part of the judge and counsel to draw jurors' attention to such issues in relation to the communication process as mediated through the interpreter.

Problems which may exist concerning cultural awareness issues cannot be altogether offset by the interpreter's contribution, however competent. Judges have a responsibility to ensure that jurors are sensitive to this area, as well as having an awareness of the role of the interpreter and the fact that even people who speak some English are entitled to interpreting services.

Court personnel

Apart from magistrates, justices' clerks and court clerks/legal advisors, already described, interpreters will meet a variety of other practitioners in a criminal court (magistrates' or Crown). Barristers (or 'counsel') and solicitors have rights of audience in magistrates' courts, although it is predominantly local solicitors who work in these courts – usually specialising in criminal work, much of which is paid for out of legal aid. Barristers and sometimes Queen's Counsel (senior barristers) are more likely to be encountered in the Crown Court, where solicitors have some rights of audience.

A duty solicitor scheme operates at most magistrates' courts in order to ensure the presence of a solicitor who gives preliminary advice to otherwise unrepresented defendants. This is paid for out of public funds. There are comparable duty solicitor arrangements in relation to police detention/custody: see p33. The role of the probation officer (described in Chapter 5) includes writing and presenting written pre-sentence reports (PSRs) and providing information about a bail hostel or bail information scheme.

Court ushers, usually identified by their black gowns, assist the court and public by calling on cases and taking care of the smooth running of the court lists generally. The usher is the first person to whom the interpreter is likely to go for information about the court list of the day and the room allocated to the case for which he or she has been engaged.

In the Crown Court the judges are experienced legal practitioners, mostly barristers, although solicitors can be appointed circuit judges after completion of three years' service as recorders. The judge supervises the conduct of the trial (hence the name 'trial judge') and ensures that the legal rules are adhered to; decides any legal issues which arise during the trial, eg concerning the admissibility of evidence; sums up the evidence to the jury (the main factual points) and guides the jury on the law; and passes sentence following a plea of guilty by a defendant or a verdict of guilty by a jury.

In the Crown Court a chief clerk is responsible for the management and general running of each Crown Court centre, for listing and for scheduling cases, calling and swearing in jurors, looking after witnesses ('witness care') and, for example, for the payment of fees for interpreters. In court, a member of his or her staff acts as a court clerk, including putting the indictment to the accused and generally dealing with day-to-day matters affecting the case. Unlike the position in the magistrates' court, the court clerk does not have to be a qualified lawyer and does not perform advisory, legal or judicial functions in relation to the trial.

Court sessions, other than in exceptional circumstances, are open to the public. Similarly, there is free reporting by the printed and electronic media, subject to certain special restrictions.

The higher courts
Other courts dealing with criminal cases are the High Court, the Court of Appeal and the House of Lords. According to the circumstances, criminal proceedings can progress to these courts on appeal. Whilst they feature prominently in any explanation of the entire courts system, these higher courts deal with only a tiny proportion of the total criminal caseload. Because interpreters rarely appear there, they will not be dealt with here. Readers who require further information are referred to the books mentioned at the end of this chapter.

Civil courts: a note
Civil cases involve disputes arising out of private disagreements, often between individuals, firms or organizations. Courts dealing with civil matters include local county courts (eg debt recovery, landlord and tenant disputes, injunctions to prevent unlawful activities and family matters), the magistrates' family proceedings court (which shares jurisdiction with the county court and High Court in relation to certain family cases and child welfare), and the High Court which deals with a wide range of private rights. The High Court also exercises a

supervisory jurisdiction, including power to conduct a judicial review of the proceedings of lower courts, tribunals and public authorities or officials who act unlawfully. The Court of Appeal and House of Lords hear appeals in civil matters. As already indicated, the underlying principles for interpreters are the same whichever court they are working in.

Interpreting in court – the legal position

As explained in Chapter 1, linguistic ability is a complex matter. People may understand some English yet be unable to cope with the kind of language used in the legal setting; or they may not be able to express themselves readily in English. Ever since *R v Lee Kun* (1916), courts in England and Wales have accepted that – even when a defendant who does not understand English is represented by a lawyer – the evidence *must* be interpreted. Many English-speaking nations still rely on *Lee Kun's* case in deciding what their own courts must do.

The question considered in the *Lee Kun* appeal was whether a legally represented defendant who does not understand English can be properly convicted when the evidence for the prosecution has not been interpreted to him or her. As was standard practice at the time, when Lee Kun, who had very little understanding of English, was charged at the police station with murdering his lady friend, the charge and his reply *were* interpreted. At a preliminary hearing, the evidence was also interpreted. However, at the trial itself, since Lee Kun was represented, the evidence was *not* interpreted, this then being the general practice. The unfairness of this state of affairs, where the prosecution evidence was not interpreted for the non-English speaker, 'never occurred' to his counsel – until the verdict of guilty *was* interpreted and his client said, in Chinese, 'Who is the witness?'.

When the Court of Criminal Appeal considered the matter, it concluded that although the omission was not an irregularity which vitiated the proceedings – since the defendant had heard the evidence at the preliminary hearing and was represented at his trial – nevertheless 'the safer, and therefore the wiser, course' was for even a legally represented defendant to have the evidence interpreted to him or her. While the death sentence was upheld, since 1916 the law has been settled and all non-English speaking defendants, whether represented or not, have been entitled to interpretation of all the evidence in criminal proceedings against them. in Parliament in 1991, the provision of interpreting in the courts was deemed to be a matter not for legislation but for *organization*.

As a party to the European Convention for the Protection of Human Rights and Fundamental Freedoms (1950) (ECHR), the United Kingdom is bound by the following obligations:

- all people who are arrested must be informed promptly, in a language which they understand, of the reasons for their arrest and of any charge against them
- all people charged with a criminal offence must be informed promptly, in a language which they understand and in detail, of the nature and cause of the accusation against them.

The above points are addressed by the Police and Criminal Evidence Act 1984 (PACE) and its Codes: see Chapter 2. People must also, under the ECHR:

- have adequate time and facilities for the preparation of their defence
- be allowed to defend themselves in person or through legal assistance of their own choosing or, if they do not have sufficient means to pay for legal assistance, they must be given it free when the interests of justice so require
- be able to examine or have examined witnesses against them and to obtain the attendance and examination of witnesses on their behalf under the same conditions as witnesses against them
- have the *free* assistance of an interpreter if they cannot understand or speak the language used in court.

This last point is dealt with in section 17 Administration of Justice Act 1973, a provision introduced to improve the law relating to interpreters in criminal proceedings and to remove the possibility of a technical breach of the ECHR.

Welsh-speakers in Welsh courts
From 1535 to 1942, English was the only language which could legally be used in Welsh courts. The sixteenth century legislation was repealed by the Welsh Courts Act 1942, according to which Welsh could be used in any court in Wales by any party or witness who considered that 'he would otherwise be at any disadvantage by reason of his natural language of communication being Welsh'. A bilingual Welsh/English speaker still had no *right* to speak Welsh in a Welsh court. The Welsh Language Act 1967 appeared to be a victory for Welsh speakers in Wales, but courts proved reluctant to give a broad interpretation of the 1967 Act, even though Lord Justice Edmund-Davies indicated extra-judicially that all who speak Welsh have 'the right to use it without let or hindrance in legal proceedings, however complete their facility in English'.

Under the Welsh Language Act 1993, all parties, witnesses or other people who wish to do so may use Welsh in *any* legal proceedings in Wales, subject – in the case of proceedings in courts other than a magistrates' court – to appropriate notice being given to the court. The position thus differs from that in other parts of Great Britain, in that people who *can* in fact speak English have the *right* to insist on using Welsh if this is their preferred language. What they say will then need to be interpreted into English unless the entire event is conducted in Welsh. 'All-Welsh trials' do occur in areas of Wales where all the participants are Welsh speakers or have a preference for Welsh – a practice which in addressing one issue might be argued as offending principles of 'open court' and infringing the Act's principle of *equality* between Welsh and English, if observers who can only speak English cannot follow the proceedings.

Over time, several initiatives have occurred in an effort to enhance proceedings in the Welsh Courts:

- the Lord Chancellor has, by way of concession, agreed that courts should submit interpreting schemes to the Welsh Language Board, as other public bodies are required by law to do (courts are not within the Act's definition of 'public body'). At the time of writing (August 1996), this is still largely at the discussion stage with court officials. The concession does, however, indicate a commitment to proper compliance with the 1993 Act.
- electronic simultaneous interpreting facilities (pp18-19) are available at some Crown Court centres. Portable equipment can be 'borrowed' by other courts.
- whilst court records and internal documents are kept in English, transcripts or copies of documents are conventionally made available in Welsh (by producing them bilingually on request) where such documents serve some further public purpose, eg so that advice can be taken concerning an appeal.
- it is planned that all documents affecting proceedings in magistrates' courts will be in Welsh and English by January 1997, unless courts positively opt for English only when generating these by computer. At present, the issue of translation arises if a Welsh speaker receives documents in English only.
- historically, fixed fees have been paid to interpreters into and from Welsh (it can be argued that this involves singling out Welsh for special treatment). The rates are £106 per full day and £53 per half day (LCD Circular (93)3). These fees should be increased to allow for any significant travelling time involved: up to £126 and £63 respectively. On fees elsewhere, see p100.

The *application* of the right in the 1993 Act can produce practical difficulties for the administration of justice, such as when Welsh is required without notice in a magistrates' court, or the possible conundrum when a witness who only speaks English is called in an otherwise 'all-Welsh' trial. There are no easy solutions. Thus, for example, insisting on notice that Welsh is required may be unacceptable to those people who consider the use of Welsh an intrinsic part of their heritage. One way forward which could prove acceptable on all fronts would be if high-quality simultaneous interpreting were provided for *all* legal proceedings. This would probably be more cost-effective and efficient, and serve the interests of justice in the long run. Current developments thus appear to be moving in the direction envisaged in the early 1970s by Lord Hailsham, the then Lord Chancellor, when he indicated that he was taking steps to provide in the short and longer term an adequate corps of interpreters, and to encourage the use of simultaneous interpretation. The aim was to set up a panel of interpreters conversant with legal procedure and terminology and capable of interpreting fluently and accurately into and from Welsh (*The Magistrate*, September 1972).

Modern technology can also partially resolve two obstacles to the use of Welsh in the courts: the shortage of Welsh-language court reporters, and the need for an English-language version of Welsh-language proceedings which are being appealed to a higher court. The use of microphones and efficient tape-recording enables subsequent transcription of proceedings. Word processing contributes to the efficiency of any translation task. In both processes, however, as in the case of interpreting during proceedings, the human element remains paramount.

PART II: INTERPRETERS IN COURT

Many considerations affect interpreters in the court situation. The items selected for inclusion in this part are among the more significant.

Engaging an interpreter
If it is correct that a party has responsibility for its own witness, a prosecutor or defence lawyer calling a non-English speaking or deaf person to testify has the responsibility for engaging an interpreter. In courts which do not regularly see non-English speakers or deaf people there may be some difficulty in arranging for interpretation. Current methods – not all of which are good practice – used in English courts include the following:

* courts' own lists of interpreters
* registers, such as the National Register of Public Service Interpreters, CACDP Directory, APCI
* leaving the responsibility for appointment to the prosecution (usually the Crown Prosecution Service)
* relying on the defence to provide an interpreter for defence witnesses
* having a duty interpreter at court
* using court employees (eg a court usher who speaks the language in question)
* commercial agencies
* local authority lists (a local authority may regularly use a particular agency or have other contacts)
* contacting the police with a view to using their list of interpreters
* contacting other public service agencies, eg the probation service
* contacting local institutes of higher education

• contacting ethnic community organizations.

Some Crown Court centres maintain their own list of interpreters and appoint directly from it, or inform an agency that an interpreter is required. Others rely on the prosecutor to make the arrangements. Enquiries of the Lord Chancellor's Department have identified conflicting information about the appointment of interpreters in the Crown Court. Interpreters for witnesses are appointed by the prosecution or defence, as appropriate.

Interpreter appointments should be well organized and the arrangements should offer effective solutions to the communication situation of non-English speakers or deaf people. The current arrangements are often more *ad hoc:*

> There is no 'framework': there is no administration in existence for providing competent interpreters. This can be damaging to the administration of justice. (Barrister)

The risk of improvisation is low-calibre interpreting, which may cost the system dearly in terms of money, time and the quality of justice. People responsible for obtaining interpreters should be aware that only a few of the sources for engaging interpreters listed above apply their own quality criteria. Some registers of approved interpreters break down their information by speciality; engagements in the courts should be offered only to those interpreters willing to do this work.

It has been held that the only person who can give evidence as to what was said in a police interview by a non-English speaking suspect is the interpreter, who heard and understood the material in the original language, whereas the evidence of the police officer who interviewed the suspect through the interpreter is hearsay: *R v Attard* (1958). The interpreter of a police interview is thus a potential witness and hence should not be engaged to interpret in the subsequent court proceedings. However, it has to be acknowledged that factors such as shortage of time (due perhaps to an overnight remand) and rarity of language may make this impractical.

The minimum information which should be provided when engaging an interpreter for a specific assignment includes:

• correct details in relation to the assignment (language and dialect, name of defendant/witness, nature of the case, likely duration, etc)
• venue, time and travel details
• contact names and telephone numbers of court personnel
• fee structures (see also p100)
• appropriate documentation.

Example of good practice
Huddersfield and Dewsbury magistrates' courts set up their own interpreter list by first advertising locally among all sections of the community and then creating a written and oral assessment process. From this, they identified competent interpreters, for whom they provided a training session in court procedures.

Court assignments

A court assignment can involve the interpreter in some or all of the following matters prior to the actual court hearing: a cell visit with the defence lawyer; an interview with the bail information officer; or a review of a pre-sentence report (see Chapter 5). The interpreter may have little preparation time.

It is vital that a meeting between the interpreter and the witness or defendant takes place before court. This session should be used to ascertain compatibility of language and dialect, provide an explanation of the interpreter's role, and ensure that the non-English speaker understands that the interpreter is impartial and will respect confidentiality. A defendant should be made aware that the interpreter will be interpreting *for the court,* and that matters of concern to the defendant should be addressed to his or her lawyer directly. Legal practitioners need to understand that interpreters do a better job if they are given advance information whenever possible. Interpreters working in the magistrates' courts need to be aware that normally the relatively fast turnover of cases in those courts does not allow time to prepare in advance and that routine or preliminary procedures can happen at speed.

When attending court, interpreters should remember to take with them all the resources they might need: dictionaries and glossaries (see below); notepad, pens or pencils and pencil sharpener. Taking 'iron rations' (sandwiches, snacks, drinks) may also be advisable.

Preparation

When first contacted by the appointing organization or agency, an interpreter should ask what the charge is, not only in order to prepare linguistically, but also to see whether the assignment is one which he or she might not wish to accept, eg a particularly nasty physical or sexual assault, or rape. Reasons for refusing an assignment include close acquaintance with the defendant or a victim. If interpreting for the defendant, the case papers should be requested in advance and read. It should be possible to obtain these from either prosecution or defence. In relation to the Crown Court, if efforts to get the papers from barristers' chambers fail, the interpreter can contact the court office to report this fact and ask for assistance. Interpreters should look at interview transcripts and pathologists' and other expert reports. When going over documents, they should draw up word lists and try to obtain the corresponding terms in the other language. Familiarity with the correct expressions improves performance and reduces strain.

Withdrawing from an assignment
Even after interpreters have accepted an assignment, they should be able to withdraw if they feel unable to do a good job, whether before or during the proceedings. Such action is costly to the courts and the parties. Proper enquiries and information at the outset (see above) should limit the need for an interpreter to withdraw from an assignment.

Arrival at court
The interpreter should be advised where to wait, where to leave his or her coat and be given a court list showing details of the charges and the name of the defendant. An element of self-confidence may be necessary on the part of the interpreter in order to find out promptly where to go and what to do.

Meetings with defendants
It is not the responsibility of an interpreter to initiate a meeting with a defendant. This should be arranged by the lawyer, if there is one, or a member of the court staff. Just as the interpreter should not be left alone with a suspect at the police station (Chapter 2), so someone else should always be present during meetings (particularly a first meeting) between interpreter and defendant.

Discussions between lawyers and their clients
Court-related conferences between solicitor and client might take place at the solicitor's office, in a prison, or in court or police cells. In the Crown Court, there may be three-way defendant-solicitor-counsel (ie barrister) conferences. The informality of such conferences can assist the interpreter in identifying the defendant's linguistic ability. Generally speaking, words and expressions that pose problems can be easily resolved at this stage. This is also the time when the interpreter can take stock of the defendant's ability to express himself or herself in his or her own language, and the extent to which he or she understands English. This is extremely important for subsequent interpreting in court. Unfamiliarity with a foreign client's background may cause difficulties for lawyers, who may not be aware of the differences between speakers of different language varieties, eg French from France, Belgium, Canada, Switzerland and the former African colonies. In an informal conference the interpreter will have to decide how much input to provide, for example in order to draw attention to relevant cultural differences, or specific issues about the client. The client may deliberately exploit his or her lawyer's lack of knowledge of his home country and tell lies, in other words trying to take advantage of the language barrier. If the interpreter is aware of this, should he or she intervene? When and how? The

client may retract his or her 'instructions', pretending that the interpreter got it all wrong. Such a 'scapegoat effect' is also not unknown to interpreters working in the international political arena.

The interpreter and lawyer should, whenever possible, find time to identify any specific terminology which might require specialist knowledge on the part of the interpreter in order to allow for proper preparation.

The interpreter's oath

In court an interpreter is shown to the witness box (usually by the court usher) and asked to give details of his or her name and qualifications and to take the interpreter's oath, either by swearing on a relevant holy book an oath such as:

I swear by . . . that I will well and faithfully interpret and true explanation make of all such matters and things as shall be required of me according to the best of my skill and understanding.

or, if the interpreter prefers, by affirming:

I do solemnly sincerely and truly declare and affirm that . . . [as above].

The interpreter has a *right* to affirm rather than to be sworn. If interpreters wish to swear on a holy book other than the New Testament, they may need to insist on using their own holy book – which might not be in regular use. Courts normally have those for the most common religions only, and it may be wise to mention this matter in advance to the court usher (and even to take a copy of the book along to court if of a less usual variety). If a particular book is not available, courts can quite properly insist on an affirmation instead.

In effect, the oath confirms the interpreter's duties. He or she is in court to enable the participants in the proceedings to understand each other properly. The wording of the oath also allows for the fact that interpretation may not be perfect at all times and that the interpreter may not understand *everything* said ('according to the best of my skill and understanding').

Witnesses

All witnesses are required to take an oath or affirm, and are then identified by name. They may be asked about further personal details if relevant, such as their job or qualifications, and whether they are neighbours or acquaintances of the defendant. The witness oath is as follows:

I swear by . . . that the evidence I shall give shall be the truth, the whole truth and nothing but the truth

and the affirmation:

I do solemnly sincerely and truly declare and affirm [as above].

Most courts have 'oath cards' and many non-fluent speakers of English are able to read the words from them adequately. In some courts, ushers ask witnesses to repeat the words 'after me'. If a witness cannot say the words properly in English, the interpreter must put them into the other language and the witness must repeat them. Witnesses may take the oath which accords with their religious beliefs and generally in whatever manner that faith provides – but, strictly speaking, it is up to them to object if handed a copy of the New Testament or Old Testament, as appropriate, to swear on (Oaths Act 1978). Alternatively, they have a right to affirm. As in the case of the interpreter (above), the court can require affirmation where it is not practicable to administer an oath according to a particular faith.

Witnesses are called by the party producing them (prosecution or defence) to give evidence known as 'examination-in-chief' (known in the USA as 'direct'). The other party can then ask questions, known as 'cross-examination'. If the lawyer who asked questions in examination-in-chief considers that matters raised in cross-examination need clarification, he or she will 're-examine'. The court itself (the judge or magistrates) may ask questions, generally reserved until the end to avoid interference. At all stages, the interpreter will, when interpreting for a non-English speaking defendant, have to interpret *everything* said, ie whispering – or, in the case of a deaf person, signing – a simultaneous version.

Objections may be raised by the opposing lawyer during the examination of a witness. An interpreter should have the relevant terminology (such as 'hearsay' or 'leading question') to deal with these situations as they arise. When lawyers engage in argument between themselves, it may be appropriate for an interpreter to indicate to the witness to wait before replying to a question to which an objection has been raised. If a non-English speaker has not understood this and answers the question, the interpreter should wait for the objection to be ruled on before rendering the reply into English.

In cross-examination, lawyers are allowed to ask leading questions (ie questions which suggest the desired answer), but not during examination-in-chief. Interpreters need to understand these basic rules and observe them. If they do not, they can unwittingly influence evidence. Here is a classic example:

Question (in English): Mr. Leclerc, what condition was your wife in when you came back to the country?
Interpreter (in French): Mr. Leclerc, was your wife pregnant on your return?
Question (in French): Yes.
Interpreter (in English): She was pregnant.

Lawyers may challenge the way in which interpreters perform. Such challenges may be perceived as personal attacks on the interpreter's integrity (criticism of the interpreter may or may not be justified). Even when the interpreter is perfectly competent, the additional time taken by *consecutive* interpretation and the barrier it erects between questioner and witness can be frustrating for a lawyer. There is considerable pressure on all witnesses during cross-examination, and lawyers sometimes use what are intended to be ambiguous or highly subtle questions. Quite often such ambiguity or subtlety cannot be conveyed in the target language. Interpreters may fail to identify the ambiguity, and will give just one meaning; or they may give all possible meanings; or be utterly confused. Lawyers should be aware of these issues and, however frustrating, be prepared to modify their style accordingly when examining non-English speakers or deaf people through an interpreter.

There is a tendency on the part of lawyers to quote the 'exact words' used by a witness at an earlier stage in the proceedings. Where that witness is a non-English speaker, the lawyer will in effect be quoting the *interpreter's* words. In order to keep confusion to a minimum, interpreters should make every effort to be consistent in their renderings in both English and the other language.

Different types of witnesses (police, expert or lay) give evidence in different ways. The court may allow police officers to consult their 'pocketbooks'. Their answers will probably be short and to the point, containing much factual information. When expert witnesses give evidence, interpreters should be prepared to deal with highly specialised terminology. The lawyer responsible for calling the expert should warn the interpreter in advance of this likelihood – since the interpreter may need appropriate preparation, as well as dictionaries, glossaries or other materials.

Ordinary, lay witnesses are likely to be more hesitant and uncertain, and their evidence may not emerge in a coherent way. Because they are unused to appearing in court, the way they give evidence normally contrasts noticeably with the way that professionals do. Unless someone (eg the lawyer who calls the witness) instructs the witness to speak 'clearly and not too fast because there is an interpreter in the court and notes of the evidence are being taken by the clerk' the interpreter may be faced with such problems as the witness:

- speaking indistinctly
- speaking too fast
- speaking very softly
- using slang.

Lack of familiarity with the person and subject matter is felt by many interpreters to be a major difficulty: 'It's like going in cold.' It is useful if enough time is made available to read through the proof of evidence or statement before the proceedings start. There must always be brief contact between interpreter and witness, to establish whether there are any linguistic difficulties (such as regional accents), hearing problems, vision problems and so on.

It is neither wise nor fair to expect the interpreter to chaperone a witness outside the courtroom, either when waiting to give evidence, or during adjournments: the witness may give the interpreter unwanted information, and the interpreter is entitled to approach the proceedings at a distance and free from any anxieties or pressures affecting the witness.

Spelling out the witness's name

The interpreter may need to spell out the non-English speaker's name in Latin characters to the court, probably in consultation with the individual. Naming conventions in other cultures may differ from English ones, and it is necessary to clarify this with the individual concerned. Many countries have an identity card containing the 'standard' name for dealing with that country's bureaucracy or authorities.

When appropriate, the interpreter can record witnesses' personal details in advance on separate sheets and hand these over to the court as the need arises.

The defendant in criminal proceedings

When the non-English speaking defendant in criminal proceedings is called to the witness box, the interpreter's work changes significantly from the situation where he or she has been sitting next to the defendant in the dock interpreting what witnesses say. Until this point, interpreting has been from English into the defendant's own language (ie working one way only), probably using the whispered simultaneous technique (see p19). The interpreter now has to interpret not only from English into the defendant's language, but also from the other language into English (ie both ways). In addition to the whispered simultaneous technique, the interpreter will be working into English consecutively (ie after the speaker), and speaking out loud for the benefit of people in court. Also, the interpreter is likely to be standing next to the defendant. It is helpful to an interpreter if a short break is allowed before the defendant is sworn in so that he or she can readjust.

Much of the above applies also to sign-language interpreters. However, normally the English version of the defendant's signing will be provided simultaneously, not consecutively. The sign-language interpreter will not stand in the witness box with the defendant because of the need to see and be seen properly.

As with all other witnesses, a defendant who gives evidence has to take an oath on the appropriate holy book, or affirm.

In examination-in-chief, the defence lawyer takes the defendant through the events surrounding the allegation. The prosecutor then cross-examines the defendant, and the defence may ask further questions if matters arising from the cross-examination need clarification. The court (the judge or magistrates) will then ask any questions it may have.

The interpreter needs to be alert to the possibility that a defendant to whom he or she is interpreting may:

- make comments to the interpreter on the evidence
- wish to communicate with his or her lawyer.

If this occurs, the interpreter should indicate to the court (the judge or magistrates) that there is some problem, and the court should intervene to ascertain what it is and deal with it appropriately. If the bench becomes aware that the interpreter is not giving a *complete* version of the evidence, the proceedings should be stopped in order that the source of the problem can be identified and dealt with appropriately. Unless the defendant receives a full rendering of all evidence, in essence, this is tantamount to being excluded from the proceedings – arguably in breach of natural justice.

The defendant (with interpreter) leaves the witness box after completing his or her evidence, and any other defence witnesses are called. Procedures are then as described above in relation to other witnesses, and the interpreter returns to the simultaneous whispering technique. The remaining procedures are described in *Part III* of this chapter: see *Stages in the trial of a not guilty plea* (p108-110).

The interpreter should not be expected to stay with the defendant when the court retires, but should be free to leave the dock, unless a lawyer or a member of the court staff needs to communicate with the defendant, or vice versa.

Written statements

Sometimes written statements made by a witness are produced in evidence, at which point the witness may or may not be present. These are usually statements made at a police interview, which are read out in court by the prosecutor. Preferably, the interpreter should be given a copy to work from – it is even better if there is an opportunity to produce a full translation ahead of the proceedings ready for use at court. In many instances, however, the interpreter is not even given a copy at court, and thus has to cope with what may be a fast delivery and a style of speaking which differs markedly from unrehearsed speech. Someone who reads out a written statement tends to speed up, and this can pose problems for the interpreter.

Transcripts

Transcripts of police interviews (ie written versions of everything said at interview, often 'transcribed' from a tape recording: see Chapter 2, *Interpreters and the Police*) are sometimes used in a similar way to written statements.

Problems can arise when this is done. For example, when the interpreter puts the English version back into the defendant's own language, because of a 'Chinese whispers' effect, modifications of the original words may well occur. It has been known for a defendant to protest – rightly – that this is *not* what he or she said. This difficulty can be solved by using a bilingual transcript, of which the interpreter has a copy.

An even more acute problem can arise where deaf people were interviewed at the police station through a sign-language interpreter. Other issues arising in conjunction with transcripts include the quality of interpreting at the original interview and the method of preparing the transcript (see p47).

Tape-recordings of interviews are sometimes played in court, because challenges may be made concerning the accuracy of a transcript of the interview, or about the quality of the interpreting at the interview or a subsequent translation. Where a sign-language interpreter assisted at a police interview, a video-recording should have been made. If the interpreter at the trial becomes aware of serious flaws in the quality of the interpretation at the police interview, he or she should inform the trial judge accordingly.

Documents

Since written material is often quite dense, it can be difficult to deal with on sight. Ideally, a document which is to be used in court should be identified some way ahead by the relevant legal representative and arrangements should be made for it to be translated in advance. However, because of the nature of court proceedings, where the need for a document to be tendered in evidence can arise at any time, an interpreter may well be asked to perform a sight translation, ie to produce an oral rendering. For this, the interpreter must have the confidence to know and state whether it is feasible to give an accurate version out loud there and then. If he or she informs the court that it is not (in compliance with interpreters' codes of professional ethics: see Chapter 7), he or she should not be required to do so.

If the court needs the document urgently and the interpreter is able to assist, a break will need to be arranged, and the interpreter given somewhere quiet to work, and if necessary provided with reference works, eg an English dictionary.

If the interpreter does produce a sight translation, he or she should specify that it must not be considered wholly reliable. If a written text is read out, the interpreter should be provided with a copy. Even if only a few words are to be quoted, it helps to see these in context. If given a copy, the relevant passage should be clearly marked – or the interpreter may inadvertently translate too much or too little.

Exhibits

Exhibits are physical objects put in evidence (eg the weapon allegedly used in an assault, or the goods allegedly stolen from a supermarket). Documents are sometimes classified as exhibits. Ideally, the interpreter should have advance warning of the exhibits to be produced if any complex points are likely to arise. Copies of pictures, maps, etc, should be supplied to the interpreter for reference.

Physical arrangements and positioning

These will depend on the mode of interpreting and the acoustics. Normally, when interpreting for non-English speaking defendants, interpreters will be asked to sit next to them. For practical reasons connected with his or her responsibilities, the interpreter has to 'shadow' the defendant, eg by standing and sitting whenever the defendant does so. Sign-language interpreters need to be seen by their clients, which naturally this affects their position in court: see also the general comments in relation to sign-language interpreters in Chapter 2, *Interpreters and the Police*.

It is useful (and tactful) to establish in advance whether a defendant has any hearing problems. Many people do not like it to be emphasised that they are hard of hearing, and dealing with this can be more difficult in the formal setting of a court. It should also be borne in mind that there can be a good deal of 'low noise' activity in a courtroom. Positioning may also need to be considered carefully if the defendant is hard of hearing, or a co-defendant or co-interpreter may wish not to be disturbed by the interpreter.

Seating often leaves something to be desired. Old benches are sometimes preferable to hard, modern plastic seats, which may be screwed to the floor for security reasons and too far away from the defendant. These may offer neither arm nor back support, and prevent a small interpreter from even finding foot support on the floor. Either the interpreter sits straight up and bellows out the words (much to the annoyance of other people in court), or balances precariously on the edge of the chair and whispers, leaning uncomfortably towards the defendant for the whole day. There should be a shelf or table for papers, books and water.

Obstacles to communication

It is important that all people concerned in court proceedings recognise obstacles to good communication, which tend to become magnified in the case of interpreting. These include:

- poor acoustics. These are often worse for the defendant, who may be sitting behind a security screen or high-fronted dock, and sometimes situated towards the back of the courtroom where acoustics, illumination and sightlines can leave much to be desired. The problem can be even more acute for the interpreter, who often has to speak at the same time as hearing what is being said. In contrast, arrangements are usually made for press reporters to be positioned strategically in order to be able to hear properly. Normally no amplification is available, let alone headphones with volume control. Using the right kind of technology can offset some acoustic difficulties. For example, a single interpreter using unwired transmission equipment can be heard at the same time by a larger number of defendants. In the absence of technology, the number of defendants who can effectively listen to one interpreter is two, and even then the interpreter, sitting behind them, would work under major stress, straining to hear properly, and in considerable physical discomfort as he or she bends forward to whisper into two people's ears. In the case of a multi-defendant trial where interpreting into a number of different languages is required, it is extremely distracting for the co-defendants to have several interpreters in the dock also working into other languages while they are straining to hear what their own interpreter is saying. The resulting cacophony is a severe problem for interpreters and defendants alike.

- physical barriers (eg glass panels, bars, distance, poor positioning)
- lack of amplification. Only rarely do courts provide or use amplification equipment. Amplification devices such as directional 'wand' microphones would help interpreters hear what is being said in court. So would greater awareness on the part of all speakers of the need to raise their heads and voices so that interpreters, often placed well away from the main body of the court, can hear clearly. Even where courts are equipped with microphones and loudspeakers, they are often not used.

Communication with others in court

There should be a clear means of communication between the parties in court and the interpreter. The parties to court proceedings, such as the defendant in a criminal case, may want to comment on, challenge, correct or contradict something in the evidence. This requires communication with their lawyer. If the lawyer is seated or standing near the defendant, his or her attention can be attracted more easily and communication established orally. Otherwise, it may be necessary for a note to be written to the lawyer. This can cause problems, particularly if the defendant needs help with writing the note or the interpreter has to write it for him or her. The defendant may have to tell the interpreter what it is that he or she wishes to draw attention to. The interpreter has to stop interpreting in order to listen to the defendant and then write the note. This can look bad (or even suspicious) in the eyes of lawyers, jurors or the court. It is the sort of issue which should be addressed before the proceedings start possibly by way of a pre-trial conference as suggested in Chapter 9, *Wind-Up* (p175).

An interpreter who needs to send a note to the judge or magistrates should not have to struggle to attract the attention of an usher. Nor is it satisfactory for the usher to tug at the interpreter's clothes while the defendant is giving evidence in order to communicate a message which has come the other way.

Interpreting techniques

As indicated in earlier chapters, there are two main techniques, *consecutive* (out loud after the speaker has finished) and *simultaneous* (at the same time as the speaker, normally whispered to one person): see pp18-19. In a court context, the interpreter chooses a particular technique, in order:

- to facilitate effective communication (between the non-English speaker and the other participants): this may be two-way or one-way (ie English into the other language and vice versa, or only English into the other language, depending on the stage of the proceedings)
- to try not to hold up the proceedings unduly.

When the interpreter is in the witness box with the non-English speaker or deaf person, this may require:

- in the case of evidence, giving an English-language version out loud to the court, perhaps phrase by phrase, sentence by sentence, several sentences at a time, or (preferably) the complete answer uninterrupted. The interpreter may take advantage of a natural gap eg when the speaker pauses or the court note-taker needs to catch up. Such decisions will be affected by the interpreter's own skills, memory, note-taking capacity, and ability to recognise signals (conscious or otherwise) from other participants
- in the case of a question, giving a low-volume version in the other language at the same time as it is being asked in English.

The interpreter's work in court often involves going mainly from English into the second language or sign-language. The normal technique involves whispering or signing a version to the defendant at the same time as the English speaker is talking. It may be difficult for the interpreter to *hear* what is being said, particularly in the spoken-language activity where the interpreter hears his or her own voice also. In addition, there may be rapid exchanges between the lawyers and the bench. Frequently, people familiar with procedural assumptions and conventions make references which outsiders do not catch. Experience, observation, study and prior information can help the interpreter to cope with this difficulty.

An example of the usefulness to the interpreter of familiarity with procedures can be seen from the following. It might occur in examination-in-chief that the lawyer says 'May I lead?'. This is a sign to the knowledgeable interpreter that, for a time at least, he or she can relax because the evidence is unlikely to be in dispute and may well follow the content of a written statement made by the witness at some earlier time. Interpreters may find, particularly where matters are not contentious, that they can satisfactorily deal with such question and answer exchanges by summarising. For example,

Question: Do you see a date on page five of that passport?
Answer: Yes.
Question: What is the date?'
Answer: 7 January 1990.

can reasonably be summarised in narrative form as:

The date 7 January 1990 appears on page five of the passport.

Obviously, it is even better if the interpreter is looking at a copy of any witness statement at the time.

Interpreting styles

The interpreter should reflect not just *what* the witness says, but also the *way* he or she gives evidence – for example, if the witness stumbles or makes a false start. The mood or demeanour of a witness is itself part of the evidence, and the interpreter should, without mimicking or mocking the original, try to speak in a similar fashion. The interpreter must strive to convey the same impression in English that the witness would have given to a lawyer examining directly, not through an interpreter. In cross-examination, a lawyer often places the witness under pressure in order to test his or her evidence. The interpreter will also be under pressure and must strive for the utmost accuracy in conveying all aspects of questions and answers.

Interpreter dilemmas

If an interpreter asks a witness to proceed sentence by sentence, then the interpreter is potentially interfering with the evidence. In order to avoid this, the interpreter needs to have high-level memory and note-taking skills. In the case of expert testimony, where highly technical material is involved, the sentence-by-sentence approach may be unavoidable.

Some witnesses, who understand a certain amount of everyday English, may not need or want everything to be interpreted to them. In this case the interpreter can provide a 'little help' when asked for assistance by the witness. This is known as 'stand-by' interpreting. Sometimes pressure may be brought to bear on such witnesses (even by their own lawyer) to testify in English. The result can be disastrous. People who do not speak each other's language *fluently* are often at cross-purposes if they try to communicate without a competent interpreter.

A defendant who has just sailed through examination-in-chief in English without a word of prompting from the interpreter is not necessarily 'shamming' when, in cross-examination, he or she needs an interpreter. The more pressured style of cross-examination can heighten linguistic difficulty.

The cross-examination of police and other officers may be highly technical, with special terms being referred to at high speed. The court interpreter thus needs to be familiar with police and related procedures. In addition, the interpreter needs to understand, be able to identify and correctly put into the target language references where the same word may be used to mean different things, eg 'caution', 'formal caution', etc. It may be appropriate to also repeat the English term after paraphrasing or giving the meaning in the other language. However, if every time a lawyer or police officer refers to 'PACE', the interpreter has to give the complete term in the other language – and then the English equivalent – he or she will run out of time if working simultaneously. In spoken English, the standard reference is almost bound to be 'PACE Codes', instead of the full expression of 'Codes of Practice under the Police and Criminal Evidence Act 1984'. For a German speaker, however, unfamiliar with the abbreviation or the reference, the full version would have to be given – 'Die gesetzlichen Verordnungen des Gesetzes von 1984 über Polizei und kriminelle Beweismittel'.

Deaf and hearing-impaired people: the legal position

In the seventeenth century, deaf people of noble birth could inherit property and bring legal proceedings if they could communicate with the legal authorities. They normally did this in writing. Deaf people from less privileged backgrounds and who were illiterate had to demonstrate to the court that they could understand the purpose of the proceeding and could communicate effectively with the court. Forms of sign language had often developed in family or other settings, but more or less standardised sign language did not develop until modern times. The sign-language based education that evolved in the eighteenth and nineteenth centuries was effective in teaching communication skills to deaf pupils, making them as adults effectively competent in a legal sense.

In law, a person charged with an offence is asked whether he or she pleads guilty or not guilty. Without assistance, somebody who cannot *hear* and/or *speak* cannot plead. Some people who *can* hear may choose not to plead. The law had to develop ways of distinguishing between these two possibilities. For this purpose, a distinction was drawn between somebody who was 'mute of malice' – who deliberately refused to plead, and the person who was 'mute by visitation of God'. Those in the first category could not escape trial simply by remaining silent. In early times, they were tortured to make them speak; later, they were simply considered to be pleading guilty, and judged accordingly; by the

92

early nineteenth century, they were held to be pleading innocent, and stood their trial in the usual way.

The law had a problem with deaf people, since it could not communicate with them in the usual – oral – fashion, because these people could not hear what was being said against them, nor (normally) defend themselves against the charges. Usually, therefore, the court adopted a compromise: because some deaf people were charged with an offence, but could not understand the proceedings, the law did not try them, but ordered that they be 'detained at the Sovereign's pleasure' – ie, confined in an institution indefinitely. If, however, the court was, exceptionally, convinced that the deaf person could understand the proceedings – whether through lipreading, or writing, or an interpreter – then it would agree to try that person in the normal way (*R v Steel* (1787)).

In the 1870s a shift occurred in attitudes to educating deaf children, away from using sign language and towards oralism – encouraging (or forcing) deaf people to try to speak. The result was a steep decline in literacy and other educational attainments on the part of the deaf community. At the same time, a paternalistic approach to deaf people developed, with social workers often playing a dual role as interpreters. As late as 1909 a judge noted that it was repugnant to consider trying a deaf man who could not speak – and then turned down the applicant's request to be released from jail after many years of confinement, at the Sovereign's pleasure (*R v Governor of HM Prison at Stafford, ex parte Emery* (1909)).

Today, British Sign Language (BSL) interpreters are available to work in legal situations, and assuming that they are competent and can communicate effectively with the deaf defendant or witness, trials involving deaf people can be held without difficulty. People who have become deaf late in life and have not learned BSL may need other assistance, such as computer-assisted transcription (CAT or 'Palantype' – which for many years allowed Lord Ashley to play an active role as a member of Parliament) or a lipspeaker, who repeats what is said so that the deaf person can lipread more efficiently.

Problems can and do still arise. They tend to occur above all in the area of availability of suitably qualified interpreters or lipspeakers, and their working conditions. Professional organizations involved with advancing communication with deaf people have been pushing for higher quality services in the courts, and in particular for two interpreters to work on any one case so that they can take turns, reducing fatigue and improving accuracy. Unforeseen circumstances have, on occasions, prevented an interpreter engaged for a case from getting to court. This is what happened in the case appealed in *R v Kingston-upon-Thames Magistrates' Court, ex parte Davey* (1985). The magistrates had decided to proceed nevertheless, on their understanding that the deaf defendant could in fact lipread. When the case was appealed to the High Court, Lord Justice Watkins observed:

Whilst acknowledging that the justices with the best of motives acted as they did, I feel bound to say that justices who go on with the hearing of a charge against a defendant who is handicapped, as this one was and is, take a very considerable risk of the hearing which they conduct being described as contrary to natural justice. There should not, in my judgment, be an occasion when a man so handicapped should be without assistance either from an interpreter or legal representation, or if need be both.

The High Court concluded, however, that whilst it saw 'the need to criticise the justices for going on in the circumstances', it was nevertheless bound to deny the applicant relief, seemingly on a quite different point.

In the case of *R v Ragu Shan* (1995), the sign-language interpreter had been assured by his professional organization that he would be working in a two-person team. On the day of the hearing, however, the other interpreter failed to appear and the interpreter present in court refused to work on the grounds that his organization had instructed him under no circumstances to work on his own. The judge hearing the case – which had already been considerably delayed for reasons unconnected with interpreting – considered sending the interpreter to jail for contempt of court, and also recommending that the government funding of the professional organization in question (CACDP) be reconsidered.

The general principle applicable in such cases was stated by Salmon J in *R v Sharp* (1960) as follows: 'It is repugnant to our sense of justice and fair play that a man who is really unable to plead and unable properly to stand his trial should be put upon his trial.' This principle was not in dispute in *Davey*, nor in *Ragu Shan*. The issues at stake here, as in many other cases which appear before the courts on a daily basis, involve the *practicalities* of interpreting arrangements – the application of the principle.

Sign-language interpreting in court

Sign-language interpreting in a court setting is subject to special factors. For example, during the examination of witnesses a hearing interpreter works one-way into English in order to give the defendant a complete version in his or her language. For a deaf defendant, the interpreter will be signing constantly. The deaf person will tend to tire more readily than the non-English speaker, because of the visual effort required. Similarly, sign-language interpreting is *physically* more tiring than its spoken-language counterpart.

People who do not understand the nature of communication through sign language are unaware of the special features which exist compared with spoken-language communication, such as the 'speaking frame', the need to maintain lines of sight, the importance of appropriate lighting conditions, and the vitally important issue relating to the specifics of any information which is signed (the *type* of window that was broken, whether someone was left-handed or right-handed, the *kind* of weapon, *where* people were standing, *how* cars collided, what *kind* of assault, etc). From what is said in court, the interpreter needs to build up a 'picture' of where and how something happened. Without accurate information, this 'picture' may be wrong, and consequently the information relayed visually to the sign-language user misleading. The interpreter may or may not realise what information is missing or what would be helpful. The court and lawyers should be alert to the interpreter's and the deaf person's needs in this regard.

Legal argument

Disagreements between lawyers concerning the exact legal rule in a given situation can arise at any time in any court. There are no guidelines about how much of this to interpret, although it is difficult to see how a party (as opposed to a witness) can fully participate in proceedings unless at least the gist of any such disputes and their outcome is interpreted to him or her. In the Crown Court, legal argument may be put to the judge in the absence of the jury, and the judge may hear some preliminary and other items affecting the course of the case 'in chambers'. The non-English speaking defendant and interpreter will be present. The judge will give a ruling. There are no such arrangements in the magistrates' court, where legal argument will take place in open court and before the magistrates.

Legal argument is a particularly difficult item for non-English speaking defendants, because they are likely to come from countries which do not have a common-law system. Lawyers do not generally take into account the presence of lay people or modify their language accordingly and tend to address each other in 'legalese'. Considerable expertise is required of interpreters during such material. Defendants should have the opportunity to follow the argument and to be aware of the implications, because they may want to instruct their lawyer.

The possibilities of legal argument are so wide-ranging that no interpreters (unless themselves lawyers) can expect to understand fully (as opposed, say, to a degree of familiarity, from experience, with legal terms and methods) everything that might be referred to in discussions. They will be obliged to listen until the subject matter has been understood (ie 'pick up the thread of the argument'), and then give an intelligible summary. If the lawyer, judge or legal advisor speaks clearly and is articulate, it may be possible to interpret simultaneously.

Interpreters should listen for any indications that there will be legal argument and ask for relevant information. The ideal preparation for interpreters is for lawyers to supply skeletal arguments and copies of legal authorities. To enable interpreters to cope, they should be provided with a copy of all texts referred to and advance notice of the arguments. Failing this (since legal argument can arise at any moment without warning), then in relation to all but the most straightforward points, the lawyer should give a short oral summary to the interpreter (eg 'I am going to submit X, quoting the law reports of cases A and B', possibly adding '. . . and I believe that the other party will argue Y').

Interpreters need not panic if legal argument is difficult to follow or interpret. They should continue to listen. Lawyers tend to repeat their arguments when 'thinking on their feet'. If the interpreter is only able to summarise rather than to interpret everything, the relevant lawyer or the court should be informed so that any necessary decision can be made regarding the amount of information which has been relayed.

If the speed at which argument is delivered is too fast and the interpreter feels that the defendant has not understood, this should be pointed out as soon as practicable. Generally speaking, interpreters should avoid standing up in the middle of a submission and saying 'I can't hear (or understand) . . .'. A note can be sent to the judge or magistrates. However, if the problem is *acute*, the interpreter should,, at an appropriate moment, stand up and inform the judge or magistrates directly that there is a problem. The interpreter might say 'For the record, I wish to draw attention to . . .' or, 'I wish to draw the court's attention to . . .'. The court should note down what the interpreter says since it may be relevant to a later claim that the defendant could not understand the proceedings.

Interpreter visibility

An interpreter sitting next to or behind a defendant in the dock, or standing next to a witness in the witness box, can be readily identified as an extra body in court. When the interpretation is provided discreetly, eg by being whispered into the defendant's ear, participants may find it easy to ignore the presence of the interpreter. However, when the interpreter has to speak up in open court, this naturally draws attention to the interpreter as a separate participant. Indications of difficulties and requests for clarification from the interpreter similarly draw attention to the interpreter.

Sign-language interpreters are particularly conspicuous. They need to be where they and their clients have a good view of each other. They might therefore have to turn their backs on the judge or jury or magistrates as they stand or sit in front of their client. To the uninitiated, this can give a negative impression which may reflect badly on the person receiving the sign-language interpreting service. In addition, particularly at the beginning, some participants in legal proceedings may be distracted by the signing.

The bench (magistrates and judges) should themselves be aware of all the practical issues relating to the provision of interpreting described in this book. In the Crown Court, judges should provide suitable explanations and instructions and instructions to jurors in order to avoid misunderstandings about the role and status of both spoken-language and sign-language interpreters.

Making notes
An interpreter must have the ability to use note-taking in the consecutive technique, yet notes can be regarded with suspicion by the parties to the proceedings and other people in court, who may view them as a sign of incompetence, affecting their attitude to what the interpreter says. Many interpreters, though able to use notes, thus feel inhibited about doing so. Figures and names, which are linguistically empty of any connotation, are difficult to memorise. It is advisable and extremely useful to jot them down.

Term banks and glossaries
Even the simplest cases can involve complicated words or terminology, often of a specialist nature: see also the reference to evidence by expert witnesses under the heading *Witnesses,* p84). Specialist dictionaries or glossaries are often indispensable. Generally, interpreters will find a bilingual personal term bank or glossary invaluable for quick reference.

Post-hearing stages
An interpreter may be asked to assist in a variety of ways after a hearing is finished and before leaving the court building:

• follow-up discussions, eg between lawyers and clients

or where the defendant has been found guilty:

• a preliminary assessment of whether there should be an appeal
• accompanying a defendant in a criminal case to discuss an appointment with a probation officer (Chapter 5) or to the fines office.

Neutrality
Issues arise where an interpreter brought in by either party is challenged by the other side, notably where an interpreter for the defence in a criminal trial is challenged by the prosecutor. So far as practicable, such issues need to be resolved before the hearing.

How many interpreters?
Where several people (witnesses and/or defendants) involved in the proceedings need an interpreter for the same language, there can be funding pressures to make do with one interpreter. If this happens, the court must be aware that in the absence of appropriate technology, it can be extremely difficult to ensure that all those who need interpreting are served appropriately.

Coping strategies

A trial – particularly a long trial at the Crown Court – can be a 'marathon' for the interpreter. He or she is required to make full and flexible use of all available interpreting techniques, and is generally assumed to have a sufficient understanding of the subject matter and the proceedings. Interpreters must be able to pace their energy and concentration, which are usually expected to last for an undefined period. A rest is rare, in the court room or outside of it. Interpreters will thus need to identify moments during which they can 'take a breather'.

In a long trial the interpreter may sit in the dock doing one-way simultaneous interpreting for several days. Suddenly the lawyer says, 'I call my client' and the interpreter is expected to move into the witness box and work *both* ways, which requires a quite different technique (consecutive: p18). Whereas interpreting in the dock is relatively informal, the register (or 'level' of language) has to change to the more formal or 'proper' language of the witness box. At this point a short break (around ten minutes) should be allowed for the interpreter to readjust. If the court does not offer a break, the interpreter should request one.

Enhancing the interpreter's performance

Experience teaches an interpreter a good deal. A confident interpreter will know how to inform the court of problems which are making it difficult to work well, such as somebody who is speaking in a low voice. Professional interpreters will not hesitate to openly indicate linguistic difficulties, such as unfamiliar or ambiguous terms, and ask for assistance from the court in dealing with them. In order to facilitate the interpreting process, people speaking in court should observe the following points:

- speak at a reasonable speed
- enunciate clearly
- speak audibly
- avoid colloquialisms
- avoid acronyms, abbreviations
- avoid jargon
- avoid overlapping speech
- speak and refer to a non-English speaker or a deaf person directly ('you', not 'he')
- do not ask the interpreter questions or make comments to the interpreter, unless they relate directly to the interpreting process and then only with permission of the court.

Some further points

In addition to linguistic skills, interpreters may find that they also need secretarial and interpersonal talents, particularly when sitting next to a defendant in the dock ('Remind me I want to explain X to my lawyer'), because the defendant's psychological isolation (far worse in the case of non-English speakers) while he or she was remanded in prison has now come to an end. They have someone to talk to in their own language! Almost all day! They have their own mouthpiece full-time. Trial is actually a welcome break in linguistic loneliness. The defendant is therefore sometimes inclined to provide a running commentary for the benefit of the interpreter. This is not only distracting, but actually prevents the interpreter from hearing what is being said in court.

Lawyers are equally inclined to treat interpreters as aides or secretaries: 'Find out whether she's got a frock – these hot pants make a bad impression on the jury!' or, 'Could you hang on to the notes until the adjournment, sending me notes all the time makes a bad impression on the jury'.

In 1973, the then Lord Chancellor acknowledged the skills needed for court interpreting, which required :

. . . not only a good knowledge of the language but facility and speed in translation. It is no use just being good at the other language: you have to translate legal terms straight into actual legal terms in the other language. A mere facility of speech will not do.

Some lawyers and judges have encountered interpreting performances in court which have fallen short of such standards. At the time, legal professionals may or may not have been aware of the unsatisfactory quality of the interpretation.

Jurors or magistrates who feel that an interpreter is *not* providing reliable services may start to ignore evidence mediated through that person. Lawyers examining witnesses through an incompetent interpreter have a far harder task than if the interpreter is skilled. They are frustrated by untrained people acting as interpreters, who consider it their role to explain to lawyers what they *think* the non-English speaker is trying to say.

As a result, lawyers not infrequently instruct court interpreters to say exactly what the witness has said – to 'translate literally'. What they should mean by this is: tell me no more and no less than the speaker has said. This is a perfectly acceptable requirement. What they should *not* mean is: give me a word-for-word transposition of what the speaker has said. Because of the nature of language, if interpreters consistently 'translate literally', they quite often produce something in the other language which is meaningless, and may even be misleading. Difficulties faced by all interpreters may include:

- lack of an equivalent institution or concept in the other culture or country
- lack of an equivalent term
- unfamiliarity with the expression in the language they are interpreting from

- unfamiliarity with the appropriate term in the language they are interpreting into
- ambiguity (deliberate or unintentional) in the original.

Fees

There are many issues associated with fees, including levels, structuring, responsibility for determining fees for specific engagements, and arrangements for payment.

Interpreters appointed to attend court hearings for non-English speakers are paid out of central funds. The Lord Chancellor's Department sets discretionary guidance allowances for interpreters in the courts. In 1996 these ranged from £15 to £25 per hour. A minimum of three hours was to be paid to those employed regularly 'in this capacity'.

This area is not without its difficulties. For example, in the case of prosecution and defence witnesses, there appears to be an assumption that the cost of interpretation will be covered by central funds or legal aid, as appropriate. At the time of writing, however (August 1996) this is one of a number of issues related to interpreting arrangements in the legal system which are currently the subject of discussion in many areas of the country. Another example is the absence of a clear-cut definition of somebody employed 'regularly' in the 'capacity' of an interpreter and hence entitled to receive a minimum of three hours' fee. Likewise, the Lord Chancellor's Department fails to indicate the criteria for applying the lower or higher end of the range, which might be understood to include level of difficulty of the case, qualifications, experience, language or other factors.

In the area of sign-language interpreting, professional organizations are pressing for two interpreters to work together on longer and more complex cases in order to improve interpreting quality. The additional cost of the second interpreter is by far outweighed by the cost to the public purse of the failure of a case caused by the mistakes made by interpreters because of tiredness. Moves to shift responsibility for 'warning' (or provisionally engaging) interpreters from the Crown Prosecution Service to defence lawyers carry implications for interpreters on a number of levels, including advance warning, delays in payment and cancellation fees (*New Law Journal*, 5/19 July 1996).

PART III: COURT PROCEDURES

Interpreters in the courts need to have some understanding of certain legal procedures in order to be able to readily identify and correctly convey references to do with the system. It is impossible to explain all common court procedures in a book of this kind: for a straightforward treatment of relevant topics, readers are referred to the books listed at the end of this chapter. The examples of practice and procedure in the magistrates' court and Crown Court provided in this section should give interpreters a feel for how the system works. They also demonstrate the context for interpreting issues of which court personnel should be aware.

Magistrates' courts

As indicated in *Part I* of this chapter, many minor offences *must* be tried or dealt with by magistrates (ie 'summarily'). Other – 'either way' – offences may be dealt with by either the magistrates' court or the Crown Court following special 'mode of trial' procedures. The basic procedure (subject to any relevant *Mode of trial* considerations: see pp106-108) is as follows:

- The legal advisor/court clerk asks the defendant to give or confirm his or her personal details (name, address, in some cases, date of birth and, possibly, occupation).
- The charge (or 'allegation') is then read out (or 'put') to the defendant followed by the statutory or other provision which is said to have been contravened. If appropriate the charge will be explained in less formal or non-legal language (the interpreter being expected to interpret both versions). If the defendant was arrested and charged at a police station, he or she will have been given a charge sheet outlining the alleged offence (see p37); otherwise he or she will have had a summons setting out similar details. The text of charges can be complex, and difficult for a non-lawyer to comprehend. As a matter of good practice, interpreters should be handed a copy of the charge sheet in advance so that they can prepare properly for the hearing.
- The court clerk asks the defendant whether he or she pleads 'guilty' or 'not guilty'. Non-lawyers would probably understand 'guilty' or 'not guilty' to indicate whether somebody did or did not do what he or she is charged with. They may not understand the vital aspects of intention and responsibility which may be involved in decisions of how to plead, or the tactical consideration as to whether or not the allegation can be established by the prosecutor beyond reasonable doubt. Regardless of how many times a defence lawyer has explained these implications to the defendant, when he or she is asked 'How do you plead?' it is a natural reaction to turn to the *interpreter* – who has just asked the question in the defendant's own language – and to ask for clarification.

In addition to the legal niceties of the concept of 'guilt', further complications may arise from the absence of any equivalent in the defendant's language. Ideally, the court should be prepared to ask the lawyer whether the concept of guilt or innocence has been properly

101

explained and fully understood. This was acknowledged by the Court of Appeal in *R v Iqbal Begum* (1991): see p106.

If the plea is 'guilty':

- The prosecutor summarises the facts, and produces a written record of the defendant's previous convictions (if any), which the defendant is asked to confirm. The prosecutor will also make any appropriate application, eg for compensation to the victim and for the defendant to pay costs.
- Other documents may be involved, such as the defendant's driving licence or a Driver and Vehicle Licensing Agency (DVLA) printout showing his or her driving record. More serious matters may require a pre-sentence report (PSR), provided by the probation service (see Chapter 5), or a medical or psychiatric report – all of which may need translating or summarising according to the circumstances.
- Either the defendant or defence lawyer puts forward arguments in favour of a lesser sentence (mitigation). Courts draw a distinction between *offence* mitigation (eg reasons why the offence is less serious than might appear) and *offender* mitigation (personal factors such as health, employment, maturity, financial circumstances).
- The court asks any remaining questions and then decides on sentence: see pp110-112.

If the plea is 'not guilty':

- The case is unlikely to proceed straightaway. An adjournment may be needed (eg so that 'advance disclosure' of the prosecution case can be provided by way of a written summary of the facts of the allegation). Acceptable dates may have to be identified for witnesses to attend court. If the case is adjourned, the court will decide whether to grant bail or to remand the defendant in custody (see below). When the case resumes, the court will go through the procedural stages outlined under the heading *Stages in the trial of a not guilty plea,* pp108-110.

Remands and bail

In the main, the Bail Act 1976 guarantees a right to bail to people charged with a criminal offence who must be released by the police, magistrates' court or Crown Court pending the next stage of their case.

If the case falls within certain exceptions (eg a second murder or rape) or the court finds that one or more statutory 'grounds' exist for refusing bail, the defendant is remanded in custody (ie in the case of an adult to prison), usually for a week at a time. *Grounds* must be announced and supported by *reasons* – so that there are two distinct items which must be carefully conveyed in the other language. The most frequently used bases are that there are substantial grounds for believing that the defendant will:

- fail to surrender to custody on the due date
- commit an offence if released
- interfere with witnesses or otherwise obstruct the course of justice.

It should also be noted that the fact that an offence has been committed whilst the person is already on bail is a ground for refusing bail.

Bail can be granted subject to conditions ('conditional bail'), eg to live at a given address; to report to the police at specified times; to stay away from a specified location or individuals such as the victim, a witness or someone charged with the same matter (a 'co-accused').

Unconditional bail means straightforward bail, ie without any requirement other than to attend court at the end of the bail period. Failing this, an additional offence of 'failing to surrender to bail' is committed. A defendant breaking a condition of bail can be arrested and brought back to court. All these matters should be explained by the court. The Magistrates' Association suggested pronouncement in relation to a remand on unconditional bail is as follows:

This case cannot be dealt with today. It is being put off until . . . You must come back to this court on . . . (day) . . . (date) at . . . a.m./p.m. If you do not come on that day at that time you risk being fined or sent to prison/a young offender institution. We should warn you that if you commit an offence whilst you are on bail you will be sentenced more heavily . . . Do you understand? . . . Then you are granted bail. (As soon as you are handed a written notice about this you may leave the court.).

There is some concern about whether or not foreign nationals are being remanded in custody simply because insufficient information is available to the court when making a bail decision. A Home Office circular on bail (69/1994) states:

The decision whether or not to grant bail can be one of the most difficult with which the courts have to deal. It follows that the range and quality of information available when the decision is taken is very important.

The circular identified several findings, one of which refers to the role of the courts in not only making decisions about bail but ensuring that the defendant granted bail understands the terms of his or her bail and the terms and purpose of any conditions.

The concepts and language used in bail cases can be complex and involve a defendant in dealing with matters outside his or her experience. A further complication arises from the fact that many languages have no single word which is the exact equivalent of 'bail'. As with many expressions, the target-language term for 'remand' is likely to be a longer expression; or where there is no exact equivalent there may be a need to paraphrase, which takes longer. When working simultaneously, the interpreter then has the problem of saying all the material in the time available. The court may need to understand this, and avoid continuing whilst the interpreter is still conveying earlier material.

Understanding a bail notice (which reproduces the court decision) requires a fairly high standard of literacy. The person concerned must also understand the serious implications of failing to appear at court on the due date or of breaking conditions. An interpreter might be asked by the court or by the solicitor to provide an oral translation of the notice outside the courtroom after the proceedings. A busy duty solicitor might be tempted to leave the interpreter to deal with the matter alone, but this is highly undesirable. The court should not ask an interpreter to check details of the defendant's personal background, although this has been known to happen. An interpreter should *never* be asked to carry out functions of the court or of lawyers.

If a bail condition requires the defendant to stay at a bail hostel, it is essential that the court ensures that the person understands what is involved. The term 'bail hostel' will not necessarily be understood by the defendant. The explanation must come from the court, the solicitor or the bail information officer (a function discharged by a probation officer: see Chapter 5).

The police have power to attach conditions to police bail. The police custody officer (see p37) must give reasons for doing so. This police power does not extend to a condition to reside in a bail hostel.

Early administrative hearings in the magistrates' court

At the time of writing, early administrative hearings (sometimes called 'preliminary hearings') are at a developmental stage and are not held as a matter of course in all magistrates' courts. Their purpose is to deal with preliminary items which might otherwise delay progress once a case starts. Pre-trial guidelines anticipate that defendants will have identified a lawyer and sought legal advice; applied for legal aid (where relevant); and dealt with other documentation relating to the offence or offences with which they are charged. Nonetheless, many defendants arrive at court without having dealt with these matters. Others find it difficult to understand what they need to do, or find it difficult to deal with the system. The latter applies particularly to people with communication problems.

Early hearing schemes mean that the defendant must attend at the magistrates' court within a few days of being charged. Proceedings in the form of an interview may last for ten to 20 minutes. The court legal advisor checks, for example, the defendant's details, progress with legal aid, that the defendant has information about solicitors, and that documents will be available (eg driving licence or DVLA printout).

Special needs, such as an interpreter, should be noted if not identified already, and preparations should then be made for the hearing proper.

The Crown Court

As already explained, only purely indictable offences or 'either way' cases referred by the magistrates' court or where the accused has opted for jury trial are heard in the Crown Court. It also hears appeals against conviction and/or sentence from magistrates' courts. The objective is the same as in the magistrates' court, ie to take a plea or to hear the evidence and reach a verdict. Broadly speaking the rules of evidence and procedure are the same in both courts: see *Stages in the trial of a not guilty plea*, pp108-110. However, procedures in the Crown Courts tend to be more leisurely. By their nature, cases can often last longer, and there is a greater degree of formality – in linguistic terms the 'register' is generally higher. There are other differences, such as the fact that in the Crown Court a verbatim shorthand record is made of everything said *in English*. Similarly, terminology differs. Two examples of this are 'indictment' and 'arraignment'.

Indictment

The 'indictment' is the name given to the document containing the allegation(s) against the accused person. (The word 'indictment' is also sometimes used to describe the allegation itself, and the term 'on indictment' to describe the procedure.) Indictments may contain several 'counts', each limited to a single offence. Several people can be charged in the same indictment. These basic rules are supplemented by others, affecting the circumstances in which cases can be tried together (known as 'joinder') or separately ('severance').

Arraignment

The accused is 'arraigned' (as opposed to being 'charged' in the magistrates' court). The clerk of the court calls upon the accused person by name, reads over the indictment and asks if he or she pleads guilty or not guilty to each count in turn. At this stage, an interpreter for a defendant will be working one-way from English into the target language.

The interpreter may face linguistic, cultural and legal difficulties. The language into which the interpreter is working may not have words which parallel the way in which the English terms 'guilty' and 'not guilty' are used. The court assumes that the defendant, following explanations by his or her lawyer, fully understands the implications of a particular plea. If this is not the case, the interpreter may be placed in a difficult position. The Court of Appeal commented on this in *R v Iqbal Begum (1991)*, in the words of Lord Justice Watkins:

> It must be appreciated that a court is very much in the hands of solicitors and counsel when a plea is being entered to an indictment. The court is entitled to feel confident that before that plea has been tendered solicitors and counsel have satisfied themselves that the person arraigned fully understands what is going on, and that that person has before that time given intelligible instructions so that counsel has in the end been able to satisfy himself that the person is able to make a proper plea. If it be that the plea is guilty, that it is a plea which is tendered after proper reflection and is one which comes from a mind made completely aware of the implications of it. The failure here both by solicitor and counsel was to realise that the reason for the apparent lack of communication lay in the inadequacy of interpretation. Yet not once does it appear to have occurred to either of them to question the interpreter so as to understand whether or not he was understanding what the appellant was saying to him and whether he, the interpreter, had the impression that she [the appellant] was not comprehending the language he was talking to her.

In *Iqbal Begum*, the essence of the difficulty was that the accountant engaged as interpreter and the woman accused of murdering her husband had no common language in which they were both at ease. In fact, the appellant initially remained silent and did not plead. The main point here is equally valid for all situations involving interpreters in the legal system: responsibility for ensuring that the communication necessary in order for a plea to be properly made – as well as for justice to be done – is the responsibility of the court team as a whole, and first and foremost of the lawyers. In *Iqbal Begum*, communication between the defendant and her lawyers had clearly not taken place prior to the trial. This was acknowledged by the Court of Appeal's ruling that the trial was a nullity and its quashing of the conviction. Everyone reading this book is advised to bear the following comment in mind at all times:

> Sufficient has now been said, we think, in this case to cause anyone who is called upon to assist a person such as the appellant as a first precaution to ensure that the interpreter who is engaged to perform the task of interpretation is fully competent to do so, by which we mean is fluent in the language which that person is best able to understand.

Either way offences and mode of trial

An offence which can be tried either in the magistrates' court or in the Crown Court (such as theft or fraud, more serious drugs offences, more serious violence or public order offences, dangerous driving) is known as an 'either way' offence. The magistrates' court must decide whether the offence appears to be more suitable for trial by magistrates or trial at the Crown Court. This procedure is known as 'mode of trial'.

The magistrates decide on mode of trial by taking a provisional view on the seriousness of the offence and the differing powers of magistrates and the Crown Court to impose sentence should the defendant be convicted. The *National Mode of Trial Guidelines* (1995, HMSO) provide guidance about this decision. If the magistrates decide that the offence is more suitable to be dealt with by themselves, the defendant still has the right to elect for (ie choose) trial by jury in the Crown Court. Before the defendant so elects, he or she is entitled to advance disclosure of the prosecution case (above). The following caution is read to the defendant by the court clerk before any plea is taken:

> This offence may be dealt with by this court, or by a judge and jury at the Crown Court, who possess greater powers of punishment than are available to this court. The magistrates will first hear representations from the prosecutor and your solicitor concerning the offence(s), to decide whether this court's powers of punishment are sufficient.

The wording may vary between courts, but the substance of this communication will be the same. The prosecutor then summarises the facts of the case and the defendant (either personally or through a lawyer) makes representations. The magistrates state where they consider the case should be heard. If they have decided that it is suitable for them, the clerk reads the second part of this 'caution' and the defendant makes his or her choice:

> The magistrates have decided that the case is suitable to be heard by this court, but the final decision is yours. You can have your case heard here or at the Crown Court, but you must understand that if you ask the magistrates to hear your case and you are found guilty, you can still be sent to the Crown Court to be dealt with if the magistrates find that their powers of dealing with you are not sufficient. Do you understand? . . . Where would you like the case to be heard? Here or at the Crown Court?

If the case is to be dealt with by the magistrates, the case proceeds as described above.

Where the magistrates decide that trial at the Crown Court is more appropriate, they proceed with a view to committal for trial in the Crown Court and become known as 'examining justices'. Essentially, the committal procedure is similar to the trial of a case. So that the court can decide whether there is a *prima facie* case, witnesses are called by the prosecutor and may be cross-examined by the defence. There may also be speeches by the lawyers. However, 'paperwork' (or 'section 6(2)') committals regularly take place without live witnesses. These involve written statements which are looked at by the defence

107

before the proceedings. They may need translating for a non-English speaking defendant. At the time of writing, the committal process is under review.

The Magistrates' Association suggested pronouncement for committal to the Crown Court for trial ('paperwork committal') incorporates a statutory alibi warning and is as follows:

> The court commits you for trial at the . . . Crown Court. At that trial you may not be permitted to give evidence of an alibi or call witnesses in support of an alibi unless you have earlier given particulars of that alibi and of the witnesses. You may give those particulars now to the court or at any time during the next seven days to the Crown Prosecution Service. Do you wish to give particulars of an alibi to the court now?
> Your legal aid is extended to cover the Crown Court proceedings.
> Full [or conditional] witness orders are made for witnesses as sought.
> You will be told the date and time when you must go to the Crown Court for your trial.

Pronouncements such as these contain concentrated, specific information. Interpreters should check on particular terms and decide how best to express them in the other language.

'Indictable only' offences
Apart from those either way offences which find their way to the Crown Court, some offences are known as 'indictable only', ie they are triable only on indictment in the Crown Court (examples are murder and other homicides, rape, robbery, aggravated burglary, serious firearms offences, drug trafficking).

Stages in the trial of a not guilty plea
In England and Wales an accused person is presumed innocent unless and until proved guilty, following the decision of a magistrates' court or a jury in the Crown Court. The English system is adversarial in nature, the opposing lawyers producing competing evidence and attempting to undermine their opponent's case. The prosecutor must establish the allegation beyond reasonable doubt. Because so much hinges on the trial, the interpreter's role in court is crucial where non-English speakers are involved. If notified well in advance about a 'not guilty' case, he or she should, before the trial, be able to obtain details of the charge as well as, ideally, copies of all relevant documents such as maps, written exhibits and written statements made by witnesses (or 'proofs of evidence'). The interpreter should be specifically advised if expert witnesses are to be called so that the implications in relation to terminology and subject matter may be explored. Information should be available from the Crown Prosecution Service, or in some instances from the defence if that is the party calling the expert.

Broadly speaking, once the initial formalities are over, the stages of a trial are the same whether the case is dealt with by magistrates or by the Crown Court, with the interpreter being sworn in at an appropriate point. When the defendant is a non-English speaker or a deaf person, the interpreter is sworn in first because court procedures should not take place in the presence of the defendant without the words being interpreted (see p75). The stages in a trial can be summarised as follows:

- identification of the defendant.
- prosecution case. The prosecutor outlines the allegation(s) and then calls witnesses and produces any exhibits to support these. The sequence is examination-in-chief, cross-examination and re-examination of witnesses for the prosecution. Some evidence may be given by written statement or in ways described earlier in this chapter.
- a submission, if appropriate, by the defence that there is no *prima facie* case, or 'no case to answer' such that the allegation should be dismissed at this point without the defendant being called on to give evidence. Submissions often involve legal references, for which an interpreter should be prepared. Defence lawyers should have briefed their client about the implications of such a submission: if they have not, the defendant may – inappropriately – ask the interpreter to explain what is happening.
- assuming that the case does progress, the case for the defence: examination-in-chief, cross-examination and re-examination of defence witnesses. The defendant usually gives evidence last.
- closing speeches by the lawyers in the case, including legal argument (which may involve legal references: see above). The defence always has 'the last word' in a criminal trial.
- in the Crown Court a direction by the judge to the jury, summarising the evidence and guiding them on legal aspects. This can be extensive in a serious case which has been heavily contested. There may be similar 'reminders' to the bench in the magistrates' court if a court clerk deals publicly with legal points (although this may equally occur in private in the magistrates' retiring room – with no one but the magistrates and legal advisor present – with a short explanation being given in open court afterwards).
- verdict (by the jury or magistrates). A verdict of not guilty results in the accused person being discharged, following which there is usually an order for his or her costs to be paid from public funds. A guilty verdict will be followed by a defence speech in mitigation and sentencing (below). In the Crown Court, the jury retires to consider the evidence and to arrive at a verdict. The verdict of the jury must be unanimous. However, it is possible for the judge to accept a majority verdict, provided that at least

ten of the twelve jurors agree. This can only occur after the jury has been allowed time to arrive at a unanimous verdict, which the judge is satisfied cannot be achieved. The verdict is announced by the foreman of the jury. At this point, the interpreter works one-way from English into the other language. While the jury is out, the interpreter may initially be required to assist with communication issues between the lawyers and the defendant. Consideration must be given to the needs of the interpreter during such recesses. Care must also be taken to inform the interpreter of the impending verdict. It has been known for defendants to be left on their own, without an interpreter, when the verdict is pronounced. Some lawyers seem to take the view that their clients have enough English to distinguish 'guilty' from 'not guilty'. Some judges take the view that no matter how adequate defendants' English might seem, they must be given the opportunity of expressing their emotions in their own language at this point. Statements by the defendant (sometimes written by hand to be read out in court) are important items; rough sight translations are not satisfactory and time should be allowed to translate them properly in advance.

Sentencing

Whether the defendant has pleaded guilty or been convicted by the magistrates or jury after hearing the evidence, the prosecutor then provides the court with any additional information about the defendant, such as previous convictions and any personal information held by the prosecutor (sometimes called 'character and antecedents'). An application may be made for compensation to the victim and for the costs of the case to be paid by the defendant.

The defence lawyer will then focus on raising issues about the offence or the offender – such as his or her age or employment record, domestic matters, and post-offence conduct – which indicate that a less severe sentence might be appropriate. He or she will also deal with the most predictable sentencing options and the impact that these might have on the offender. Aspects related to disqualification (in motoring offences) or compensation to a victim may also be referred to, together with the offender's financial circumstances. Before making a speech in mitigation, the lawyer should have gleaned sufficient cultural information about the defendant (see *Conferences between solicitor and client*, p34). Lawyers should not treat interpreters as cultural informants.

Interpreters should be familiar with standard terminology and standard explanations connected with the range of possible sentences: see the handbooks referred to at the end of this chapter.

For the defendant, pronouncement of sentence by the judge or magistrates can be a highly charged moment. It is important that the judge or chairman of the bench speaks directly to the defendant, and avoids 'sentencing the interpreter'.

To facilitate this, the spoken-language interpreter can take a small step back from the defendant. This serves two purposes: distancing the interpreter from the defendant, whilst allowing the defendant to hear the interpreted version of the sentence. It is vital that the interpreter conveys accurately what the chairman says to the defendant – including any explanation, reason or 'homily'.

The powers of the Crown Court range up to life imprisonment, which is mandatory for murder, and discretionary for such offences as manslaughter and rape. Many of the more serious offences carry a maximum sentence of 14 years in prison. Maximum penalties in magistrates' courts (at the time of writing) are a fine of £5000 and/or imprisonment or detention on a single matter for up to six months (consecutive sentences can raise this to 12 months). Sentences may be made consecutive to one another, or concurrent. The main sentences are:

- imprisonment (or detention in a young offender institution for people below 21 years of age)
- a range of community sentences including probation orders, community service orders and combination orders (see Chapter 5)
- fines
- compensation (as a penalty in its own right or in addition to other punishment)
- attendance centres (for people below the age of 21)
- hospital and guardianship orders under mental health legislation
- a range of 'ancillary orders', such as orders for costs and disqualification, eg from driving, being a company director or keeping an animal.

When the court has reached a decision, the offender will be required to stand whilst the judge or chairman announces the sentence. By way of example, the following is the Magistrates' Association suggested pronouncement concerning compensation:

For the offence of . . . :
(a) you will pay compensation of £ . . . to M . . . for the injury/damage/loss caused; or
(b) you could have been ordered to pay compensation but the court cannot make such an order because . . .

Many court orders and sentences involve complex explanations which the court delivers orally, often from an announcement card or prompt. If possible, these formal texts should be made available to interpreters. Some sentence announcements involve the offender in acknowledging that he or she has understood, and in agreeing to the terms of the order. This may require the offender to answer questions such as 'Do you understand?' and 'Do you agree?'

111

(see p122). When these questions are asked through an interpreter, the court must take care to ensure that the defendant really has understood.

Before a fine is imposed, the court will assess the offender's financial circumstances (when a form will often need to be completed, unless the defence lawyer has already prepared his or her own detailed account). Alternatively, the court clerk may ask questions of the offender and these will require interpretation, as will the answers. The interpreter should *not* be the person to ascertain the defendant's financial circumstances (as opposed to interpreting any questions).

Seriousness, protecting the public and 'restriction of liberty'

Courts sentence primarily on the basis of the seriousness of the current offence and any associated offences or, in relation to sexual or violent offences, the protection of the public from serious harm from the offender. Some sentences, particularly community sentences, are assessed for their appropriateness by the extent to which they restrict the liberty of the offender (ie in the community).

In so doing, the court can consider other offences which the offender asks to be taken into consideration (TICs). Where applicable, the prosecutor will produce a written list of these, which the offender will be asked to confirm and may be asked to sign.

The court will also consider a PSR (pre-sentence report: see Chapter 5). Written psychiatric evaluations, which are language-based, are also frequently used. If they are carried out in English for limited-English speakers, it may be difficult to distinguish between a linguistic and a psychiatric cause of anomalies. The professional literature advises against using interpreters for psychiatric evaluations, for a variety of reasons. If, however, there is no alternative to using an interpreter, care must be taken to engage a professional interpreter who has experience in such evaluations.

Road traffic cases

If the offences relate to road traffic matters, the offender's driving licence will be called for. If it is unavailable, the case will be adjourned for a computer printout from the DVLA. Occasionally, an offender may be allowed to give evidence on oath, for example to the effect that he or she has a clean driving licence.

Youth courts

The youth court (which operates under the auspices of the magistrates' court) deals almost exclusively with criminal cases. It is subject to the same general laws, practices and procedures as in the magistrates' court and the Crown Court, but governed by a number of special rules. People who appear in the youth court are known as 'children' or 'young persons':

• 'children' are aged 10 to 13 years inclusive

• 'young persons' are aged 14 to 17 years inclusive.

An interpreter is likely to find the youth court environment and its procedures less formal and intimidating than those of other criminal courts. These courts must 'have regard to the welfare of the child or young person' (the 'welfare principle' contained in section 44 Children and Young Persons Act 1933). Representatives from local authority social services departments or the probation service are invariably present and supply the court with pre-sentence reports (PSRs), school reports and other assessments of the juvenile as necessary. There are special forms of procedure designed to involve the juvenile and his or her parents or guardian in the proceedings and to facilitate communication with a younger age group. Further details of these specialist items are outside the scope of this work, but readers are referred to the books listed at the end of this chapter.

If an offence is extremely serious (murder, manslaughter, etc), then the young person's trial *must* be held at the Crown Court. Other 'grave crimes' – such as rape, wounding, aggravated burglary or sexual assaults – can, depending on the nature of the offence and the age of the offender, be sent to the Crown Court for trial under section 53 Children and Young Persons Act 1933. Where its own powers are insufficient, the youth court can also commit an offender to the Crown Court to be dealt with.

Parental responsibility
There is a strong emphasis on parental involvement and responsibility. Parents or guardians are required to attend a youth court with their children under the age of 16 and may be required to attend for hearings involving 16 and 17-year olds. Courts have powers to bind over parents or guardians, or order them to pay their children's fines, and so on.

Some special linguistic considerations
Because youth court proceedings are closed to the general public, interpreters will have an opportunity to familiarise themselves with such courts only where they ask that court for and are granted permission to observe (the likely response varying from place to place).

The closer proximity between participants in youth courts may increase tensions between defendants and witnesses. The presence of a non-English speaking or non-hearing parent or guardian in youth court proceedings would make it necessary for all of the proceedings to be interpreted. Parents or guardians in a youth court usually sit next to the juvenile. In order to avoid the lengthening effect and interruptions of consecutive interpreting, simultaneous whispered interpreting should be used for non-English speakers. The presence of an interpreter, whether for the juvenile or the parent/guardian, may require the seating to be re-arranged, or the use of appropriate technology (see p173).

113

On the whole, young people learn English much more readily than their parents or grandparents. However, their knowledge may be superficial. They are likely to lack a real understanding of English legal language and procedures – in other words, they are not 'streetwise'. For example, a juvenile from outside the United Kingdom may not be familiar with the word 'solicitor'.

It is possible that, even though an interpreter has been engaged for the juvenile, the young person may wish to impress the court with his or her knowledge of English. The court should be aware that, as in proceedings involving adults, ability to speak *some* English does not in itself imply that legal proceedings can be followed properly, or that the people concerned can express themselves adequately. It is better to instruct the interpreter to interpret everything to the youngster, regardless of whether he or she speaks English from time to time. If interpreting has been considered necessary , it is far better for *all* the proceedings to be interpreted for young defendants rather than allowing them to guess or try to impress the court with their command of English.

Further information about courts and court procedures can be found in:

- *Introduction to the Criminal Justice Process* by Bryan Gibson and Paul Cavadino (Waterside Press, 1995) which provides a broad overview of the system and its personnel.
- *Introduction to the Magistrates' Court* by Bryan Gibson (Sècond edition) (Waterside Press, 1995).
- *Introduction to the Youth Court* by Winston Gordon, Michael Watkins and Philip Cuddy (Waterside Press, 1996).
- *The Sentence of the Court: A Handbook for Magistrates* by Michael Watkins, Winston Gordon and Anthony Jeffries (Fourth reprint) (Waterside Press, 1996).

CHAPTER 5

Working with the Probation Service

PART I: CRIMINAL CASES

The probation service carries out various functions in relation to criminal cases. A central responsibility is the provision of information about offenders to courts at the sentencing stage, by way of pre-sentence reports (PSRs). Other situations in which there is a need to communicate with people who may not speak English include the carrying out of community sentences, bail information schemes, and procedures before, during and after the release of offenders from prison or other custodial institutions. Many aspects of the work of the probation service are governed by National Standards. The standard governing PSRs states, explicitly, that:

> Where language differences or hearing difficulties impair effective communication between the report writer and anyone who should be interviewed, an accredited interpreter should be used. In Wales an offender should have the right to use Welsh, if necessary through an accredited interpreter. (para 7)

An interpreter's assignment with a probation officer might involve attending at:

- an interview for the purposes of producing a PSR
- an interview concerning information about bail
- a meeting or interview with an offender who is on probation or carrying out community service
- a probation hostel meeting
- a session (eg at a probation centre) connected with 'offending behaviour'
- a prison.

Engaging an interpreter
Each of the 56 probation services in England and Wales has developed its own system for engaging interpreters. Many probation services use:

- registers such as are mentioned in Chapters 2 and 4
- in-house lists of experienced interpreters
- commercial agencies.

There is an emphasis on using interpreters who are accustomed to the delicate and sensitive task of dealing with offenders or people charged with criminal offences – interpreters who are 'tried and tested' and who 'fit in'. The following comments indicate that the probation service views the interpreter as an essential part of the communication process with offenders:

> The offender might have some difficulty in understanding the concepts and the interpreter will assume some responsibility for awareness of these. The interpreter has to engage in the process. Ideally, as the interpreter becomes more experienced in the work of the probation service there should be growth in the role of that interpreter. (Probation officer)

Fees

Charges for this type of work and for a session lasting for, say, a minimum of three hours are around £24 per hour plus travelling expenses (March 1996). Commercial agencies tend to charge higher fees, with the agency interpreter actually receiving far less than the client pays the agency. Agencies are more likely to be approached for interpreters offering 'rarer' languages, such as some African languages or dialects.

COMMON PROCEDURES

The pre-sentence report (PSR)

In practice, courts request PSRs in all the more serious cases. It is particularly important to recognise the unique value of such reports in relation to non-English speakers when – via an interpreter – items may emerge which might otherwise have remained undisclosed or unrecognised due to language or cultural nuances. A PSR is compiled by a probation officer. The information contained in the report includes a summary of the facts of the offence (or offences), an assessment of its seriousness and of the offender's attitude to it, and the effect on the victim or victims. The PSR will include personal information about the offender which is relevant to sentencing, eg any special circumstances such as a family crisis, alcohol, drugs, or mental health problems. Where relevant, it will indicate the most appropriate community sentence.

If a report is required on a foreign national, the report writer considers whether or not information can be confirmed in the defendant's home country. To facilitate the gathering of information, international branches of social services departments and the Red Cross may be contacted, as well as embassies or consulates (with the permission of the offender).

Probation service guidelines on PSRs make it clear that the report must be free of discrimination on the grounds of race, gender, age, disability, language, ability, literacy, religion and sexual orientation.

PSRs have significant implications for offenders, and probation officers are aware of the need to obtain high-quality interpreters. An officer is likely to require a briefing session with an interpreter prior to conducting a PSR interview. In addition to making sure that the interpreter and the offender speak the same language and understand each other properly, topics to raise in this session might include such things as the nature of the offence (which may mean talking about sexual, violent or other disturbing matters) and cultural implications.

If a non-English speaker or a deaf person has been remanded to prison to await sentence the probation officer will normally engage an interpreter and have a short briefing session at the prison – before meeting the offender – to identify the objectives for the interview. Probation officers prefer working with interpreters experienced in prison interviews because inexperienced ones can find the environment hard to cope with. Interpreters can be vulnerable to pressure from frightened, lonely offenders, and there is an understandable temptation to offer to 'remain in touch' with a prisoner without taking full account of the potential hazards.

Another difficulty noted by certain probation officers is a judgemental response on the part of some untrained and inexperienced interpreters:

Throughout the interview the interpreter rolled her eyes in disapproval and never once looked at the prisoner. (Probation officer)

"This is a load of rubbish he's telling you, you know!" or "This doesn't make sense at all." (Interpreter)

But probation officers who have worked with *professional* interpreters find them to be effective and valuable colleagues:

It is nice to feel that the interpreter is an extension of yourself rather than a barrier to communication. (Probation officer)

Experienced and competent interpreters are used regularly, but occasionally one will arrive for an assignment very tired because he or she has been working all night. (Probation officer)

During an interview a probation officer will take into account not only the information transmitted orally but also the implications of an offender's silences and 'body language'. Interpreters need to be aware of these matters:

117

I watch for non-verbal behaviour and signs; getting underneath these and deciding what they mean is very important. If the offender is a non-English speaker or is deaf, considerable expertise is required on the part of the interviewer if 'body language' is not to be misrepresented. Working through an interpreter is likely to make the task more complex, and the relationship between the interviewer and the interpreter might well influence the quality of the report. (Probation officer)

Sex offending, child protection and domestic violence are among those issues which require considerable sensitivity and expertise during the PSR interview. Whatever the offence, an interview for a pre-sentence report which is to be conducted through an interpreter requires detailed planning and pre-interview preparation.

The PSR at court
The PSR is confidential to the court and will not normally be available to a defendant and his or her lawyer before the hearing at which sentence is to be passed. In the absence of permission from the court (which would be unusual but could be obtained by way of a special application if the PSR happened to be ready ahead of schedule), the probation officer is not permitted to release the report in advance. Under the usual practice therefore, it is unlikely that a written translation will have been prepared in advance, despite the fact that the defence lawyer needs – together with the defendant – to identify issues which will be referred to when addressing the court. Hence the interpreter has to do an 'on the spot' (ie sight) translation for the benefit of the non-English speaker. If there are no private interview facilities at the court, this exercise will have to be carried out in a public area. If the offender has been remanded in custody for sentence, this stage will occur in the court cells. Technically, there would appear to be no breach of confidence in a probation officer arranging for a written translation in advance of the court hearing if the translator is regarded as equivalent to the probation officer (or an 'extension of" – see p117) for this purpose.

Bail, bail information and bail hostels
The probation service operates 'bail information schemes' in most parts of England and Wales. The information obtained is passed to the Crown Prosecution Service (CPS) and considered by a court when making a decision about whether to remand a defendant in custody or to release on bail (see pp102-104). This can be especially relevant in relation to:

- bail conditions (where the need for high-quality interpreting has already been explained in Chapters 2 and 4)

118

- bail hostels (below): because only a court (ie, not a police officer) has the power to release a defendant on bail with a condition of residence in such a hostel.

Bail hostels are managed by the probation service and are used to accommodate people on bail awaiting trial or sentence. The probation service bail information officer will interview a defendant prior to the hearing to ascertain whether or not a hostel placement is appropriate and find out if one is available for the offender. If the magistrates' court decides to remand the defendant on bail with a condition of residence to a bail hostel, the bail information officer will inform the hostel if an interpreter is needed. From this stage on, the responsibility for providing and paying for an interpreter rests with the probation service. On arrival at a bail hostel there is an induction procedure during which the person concerned is informed about the hostel placement. Hostel rules, the individual's rights, and the night-time curfew are some of the items which are explained at this point Many hostels provide explanatory leaflets translated into a number of languages. Interpreter services are unlikely to be provided on a day-to-day basis but the larger hostels tend to employ staff with language skills who are able to communicate with residents informally. For formal interviews, or for applications for bail variations, professional interpreters are likely to be engaged. As with other areas of the legal process, financial constraints influence decisions on whether or not to appoint an interpreter.

Community orders which may require interpreting
A community order can be made by the court if the offence is 'serious enough' to warrant this. The range of orders – each individually known as a 'community sentence' and available according to age – are follows:

- probation order (16 years upwards)
- community service order (16 years upwards)
- combination order (16 years upwards)
- curfew (16 years upwards: in 1996, limited to just a few areas of the country)
- attendance centre order (under 20s only)
- supervision order (under 18s only).

Probation orders
Probation orders always contain 'standard conditions'. The Magistrates' Association recommended pronouncement for such an order is as follows:

We believe that this offence is a serious one and that the most suitable way of dealing with it is for us to order a community sentence.

We propose making a probation order. You must understand that this sentence restricts your personal freedom. We have chosen the order and how long it should last, to match as far as we can, the seriousness of your offence(s). This means that you will be supervised by a probation officer in order to:

(a) help you to change your ways; or
(b) protect the public from harm from you; or
(c) stop you offending again.

This Order is for . . . months/years. During this time you will be supervised by a probation officer for the . . . petty sessional division. You must keep in touch with the officer and tell him/her if you change your address. You must keep appointments at the probation office or at your home when required.

If you break any of these conditions or commit another offence during the period of the order you could be punished or dealt with in a different way for the offence(s) we have been considering today. If you offend again during the time of the probation order, you will be punished separately for that offence.

Do you understand?

Do you agree to keep the requirements of the order?

Very well, we make a probation order for . . . months/years. Please see the probation officer before you leave the court.

The exact words used may vary and some additional explanations might be included. The order may, if the court thinks it appropriate, contain further conditions (sometimes called 'requirements'), eg:

You will also be required to:

(i) live at . . . and/or
(ii) take part in the following activities as instructed . . . and/or
(iii) attend at a probation day centre for . . . and/or
(iv) undergo treatment for drugs or alcohol dependency.

An offender might, for example, be placed under a two-year probation order to which an 'alcohol education requirement' is added. The court will announce and explain this in outline, and seek the agreement of the offender. Outside court, the supervisor will explain to the offender in broad terms what is involved and possibly arrange a first appointment or attendance. At a subsequent session, the offender might be instructed how to set up and complete a daily diary of his or her alcohol consumption. The session leader may use a flip chart or slides and hand out written materials – all of which may have to be put into the other language. In order to transmit the information accurately, the interpreter needs to understand what the aims of the education programme are, as well as the concepts and terminology.

Community service

A community service order requires the offender to do unpaid work in the community for between 40 and 240 hours as ordered by the court. This obligation will need to be conveyed in the other language. Interpretation services might later be needed at a meeting between the offender and, say, the scheme supervisor or organizer. This demanding sentence requires offenders to understand the nature of the work and what is required, where and when to attend, and the effect of not attending. It is thus vital that the interpreter is familiar with the nature and terms of such an order. The Magistrates' Association recommended pronouncement is as follows (although the wording may well be modified locally):

We have heard all the facts of the case (and considered a report about you). We believe this offence is a serious one, and that for you the most suitable way of dealing with it is for us to order a community sentence.

We propose making a community service order. You must understand that this sentence restricts your personal freedom. We have chosen the order and how long it should last, to match as far as we can, the seriousness of your offence(s). This means that we are ordering you to do something useful for the benefit of the local community.

You will have to report to the community service organiser when directed and carry out unpaid work for a total of . . . hours during the next twelve months. The organizer will tell you exactly where and when to report, and the kind of work you will have to do.

You must tell the officer at once of any change of address.

If you break the terms of the order, or do not make a good job of the work, you can be brought back to court and fined or sentenced in some other way for the offence(s) we have been considering today.

121

You or your community service organizer can ask the court to review the order if your circumstances change.

Do you understand?

Do you agree to keep the terms of the order?

Then we make a community service order for . . . hours.

Combination orders
A combination order contains elements of probation and community service. The standard forms of announcement or explanation reflect elements of the two orders already described. As always, the interpreter has a responsibility to understand the details and to render them accurately.

Supervision orders
The probation service may also be involved in supervision orders – usually made by the youth court (see pp112-114) – although, in practice, local authority social services departments will usually take responsibility for younger children in trouble with the law. With those aged 16 years and over, day-to-day responsibility is often shared by multi-agency youth justice teams. A supervision order can only be made in respect of someone who is under the age of 18 (usually by magistrates sitting in a youth court). A supervision order is similar to a probation order, but in arriving at a decision to make the order welfare considerations come to the fore, and attempts will be made by the supervisor to involve the offender's parents or guardians in the carrying out of the order. This means consulting them and encouraging them to offer support and take responsibility – which may involve the supervisor acting as a mediator between parent and child and helping to set boundaries of acceptable behaviour to which all parties can agree. Even where the young offender speaks and understands English, parents or guardians may be non-English speakers or deaf, in which case the supervisor should discuss with the interpreter in advance ways of checking whether the parents fully understand the contents and implications of what is being said. Depending on the circumstances, the interpreter might be allowed to take some responsibility for this, but overall conduct must be retained by the supervisor.

Probation service work with prisoners
The probation service works with offenders before, during and after custody. Work inside a prison includes programmes to prepare prisoners for release. These are similar in content and style to those for offenders attending probation centres.

122

PSRs serve as a valuable resource for prison staff, providing personal details about a prisoner which might otherwise not be revealed during interviews at the prison with either an official interpreter or an inmate 'interpreter'.

Probation officers who work full-time in a prison are seconded from the local probation service but paid for out of the prison governor's budget. At the time of writing, the indications are that personnel from the probation service working in prisons are being reduced. Interpreters brought in to assist in prisons are also paid for out of the governor's budget, and there may well be similar implications in the future for interpreter services as prison governors become less and less willing or able to pay for them.

PART II: FAMILY PROCEEDINGS

A further significant responsibility of the probation service is to provide a 'Family Court Welfare Service' in proceedings in the magistrates' court, county court or High Court (the principal legal provision being the Children Act 1989). If children are caught up in such processes, courts may ask the family court welfare service to assist, for example by:

- meeting the parties before or during a 'directions appointment' for preliminary assessment and to identify areas of agreement. Directions appointments are held in private to deal with preliminary matters affecting family proceedings. Usually the parties (both parents) and their lawyers are present, as well as the court clerk in the family proceedings court, or the District Judge in the County Court. The family court welfare officer should identify the issues which are in dispute, and whether or not there is any prospect of agreement being reached.
- meeting the parties at the direction of the court in order to assist them to make agreed decisions about their children.
- carrying out enquiries and preparing a welfare report to assist the court. The Children Act 1989 contains a 'checklist' of items which the court must take into account. Interpreters should be aware of these requirements because this will assist in understanding what the assignment involves. As with most work undertaken by interpreters within the legal process, these interviews are sensitive settings and involve information which is confidential. Whilst confidentiality and impartiality are cornerstones of most interpreters' ethical codes, members of a family having a welfare report written about them need to be reassured about the professional discretion of the interpreter. This is an issue which needs to be addressed by probation services and interpreters alike.

It is in areas such as these that there is the greatest demand for interpreters by the probation service. Interpreters are often required for parents or grandparents in family groups because, unless a child is very young or has a hearing impairment, it tends to be older relatives who do not speak English. The interpreter needs a sound grasp of the purpose of interviews and of critical decisions and recommendations that welfare officers have to make, for example when recommending where and with whom children ought to live. Sessions such as those involving disputes between parents require an awareness of the sensitive matters which may be covered. The dynamics of these interviews are of significance for the interpreter, and pre-session briefings between the officer and interpreter are a vital aspect of the process.

An issue of concern to practitioners, interpreters and academics is the extent to which interpreters draw attention to cultural issues. This is a recurring theme. Probation officers need to know about cultural attitudes and behaviour with which they are unfamiliar. However, the cultural background of an individual (in effect that of a whole nation) is all too often reduced to simplistic terminology and concepts. Too little knowledge can lead to misunderstandings between an interviewer and the client. On the other hand, a brief discussion of generalised cultural information along the lines of 'women in . . . are not allowed to go out alone or to talk about sexual matters', can be just as misleading. How might an interpreter working in Brazil describe to a colleague the culture of an English family?

Specific cultural information can be helpful, but the responsibility for identifying what requires clarification should rest initially with the probation officer and not be left to the initiative of the individual interpreter. Sharing information about such matters can only be of real value if the interviewer and the interpreter develop a mutual understanding of the way each works, and what the interview is about. Pooling knowledge can be helpful.

Closely related to cultural issues is another debate: that of the 'interpreter as advocate'. Interpreters can be placed in a vulnerable position by the expectations of clients who might well expect the interpreter to put forward their case for them. In divorce proceedings the parties can be extremely emotional and turn their anger or distress onto the interpreter, who may be perceived as the person to blame for failing to communicate the message properly. The non-English speaker is more likely to be angry with someone who speaks his or her language than with the professional officer who is seen as an authority figure.

Engaging and paying an interpreter
If both of the lawyers have engaged their own interpreters there can be considerable difficulty if disputes arise between the parties, thus creating a highly charged emotional atmosphere which can sometimes be directed at the

interpreters. Similar difficulties can arise for an interpreter engaged by the probation service. Such issues should be discussed and resolved in advance.

There are limitations on the court's power to pay interpreters who are engaged to work in civil matters. As a result, an interpreter must often be brought in by the legally aided party, or at the cost of one of the parties. The interpreter may then not be perceived as occupying a neutral role:

> We have concerns about family members being used as interpreters and about pressure on parties to give the impression that they understand more than they do. We are rarely able to provide interpreters at directions appointments. It is doubtful if this is an appropriate funding demand on us, and in any event, the listing process does not identify need early enough for us to provide an interpreter. The lack of court funding is a serious matter. (Court welfare officer)

Under the prevailing rules, the county court has a discretion in civil cases as to the payment of interpreters. Legal aid may be available to cover an interpreter's fees in civil cases, but the magistrates' family proceedings court would appear to have no specific statutory authority to appoint and pay for an interpreter unless this is permissible out of central funds.

Conciliation and mediation
Conciliation meetings take place between the parties and a court welfare officer with the objective of helping parents to reach an agreement which is in the best interest of the child or children. An interpreter present at the meeting must understand that whatever is said is confidential to the extent that the matters under discussion will not even be revealed to the court unless all the parties agree. Methods of communicating with parents in these circumstances require special sensitivity and awareness on the part of the interviewer and the interpreter. The trained interviewer will adopt appropriate strategies for dealing with people under stress and the interpreter needs to understand and reflect these.

PART III: PROBATION SERVICE INITIATIVES

The following are a few examples of probation service initiatives:

MIDDLESEX PROBATION SERVICE
As noted earlier in this chapter, gathering information for a PSR on a non-English speaker invariably requires the assistance of an interpreter. The Middlesex Probation Service has, over a long period, developed its own list of interpreters. Many of the people on the list are members of the

Association of Police and Court Interpreters (APCI) and of the Institute of Translation and Interpreting (ITI). When a rare language is required for which no interpreter is listed, commercial agencies are contacted.

In 1994 Nicholas Hammond, a probation officer serving with the Middlesex Probation Service and in March 1996 at the Foreign Nationals Unit in Uxbridge, conducted research into the value of pre-sentence reports on foreign nationals. A number of his findings, which were reproduced in a report, are referred to below (with permission). Of those foreign nationals not normally resident in the UK who are arrested, many are apprehended at ports of entry for Customs and Excise offences – principally drug importation. Although the Criminal Justice and Public Order Act 1994 removed the mandatory PSR, courts continue to request them. The former requirement that a PSR must be considered by any court before imposing a custodial sentence in respect of virtually all offences resulted in reports being written on non-UK residents which would probably not have been before. This provided new material for analysis:

> Few of the judges interviewed could recall previously adjourning sentence for the preparation of a report on drug importation offences.

Hammond interviewed a number of foreign nationals awaiting sentence to ascertain the importance of contact with the PSR writer:

> This contact could include seeing them in the cells on their first appearance at a magistrates' court and on subsequent remands, at prison support groups, and at interviews arranged specifically for the purpose of report preparation. General advice about the criminal justice system, legal process, prison regime and the sentencing process were areas where the report writer was felt to have been particularly useful. This was a particular concern of foreign nationals who had limited or no use of English.

Research into the attitude of convicted prisoners awaiting sentence revealed some doubts about the impact that a PSR would have on the outcome, but even those who expressed such a doubt were reassured by the fact that a report had been prepared on them:

> There were graphic descriptions of how a foreign national's experience of being arrested and processed through a foreign criminal justice system had made them feel frightened and isolated, and reduced to a name, number and drug weight.

The majority of those interviewed felt that the criminal justice system discriminated against them and sentenced them more harshly because they were foreign nationals.

When assessing the value of PSRs on foreign nationals, liaison probation officers felt that they were primarily important and justified because they enabled a disadvantaged and marginalised group within the criminal justice system to receive attention and support.

The lack of opportunity for a defendant to discuss the report with the barrister in their case prior to the court hearing was found to have caused particular problems for non-English speakers:

Amongst those foreign nationals where an interpreter was used, it was unusual for them to have more than a cursory description (of the report) given to them.

I will see PSRs on the morning of the court. Generally foreign nationals are so nervous that I don't think they really take it (the PSR) in. I think that there is arguably a fault in the system that we get them so late in the day, and I say that from the point of view of the client and advocate. (Barrister)

The professionals felt that despite the widespread variation in the use of the PSRs, there were clear advantages to preparing them:

Liaison probation officers felt that PSRs had broken down some of the stereotyping of foreign nationals and enabled the court to view them as individuals, with their own unique history, background and reason for their actions.

In summarising his research, Hammond noted the consensus that PSRs were of good quality and of value to the foreign national. It is clear, not only from the findings arising from this research, but also from the observations of many other probation officers as well as interpreters themselves that interviewers and interpreters need to continue developing their skills in the preparation of PSRs on non-English speakers.

INNER LONDON PROBATION SERVICE
In 1990 the Inner London Probation Service (ILPS) published a report based on research conducted by Ayesha Tarzi and John Hedge. Ayesha Tarzi is employed by ILPS as its foreign offenders co-ordinator. The study, entitled *A Prison Within a Prison*, examined in detail the problems and needs of foreign prisoners, considered options and provided recommendations for improving

services to them. The report identified implications, not only for the probation service, but also for lawyers, the police, courts, embassies and the prison service. Subsequently, the Inner London service initiated a number of schemes with the purpose of raising standards for the provision of interpreter services.

The use of interpreters in ILPS is based on its commitment to offering adequate service to non-English speakers. Probation officers have multi-national client caseloads and frequently use interpreters across a wide range of languages. In addition, many of the service's information documents are translated into at least 15 different languages.

The experience of ILPS, in common with other probation services, is that in order to communicate with non-English speaking individuals, officers seconded to prisons invariably have to make use of bilingual prison staff or use the services of another inmate chosen or suggested by the prisoner: see, generally, Chapter 6.

A comprehensive set of guidelines relating to the use of interpreters has been prepared by the foreign offenders co-ordinator, together with a *Resource Guide* listing experienced interpreters and translators, which is available for reference by probation officers.

The Family Court Welfare Service of ILPS has also produced a paper on the use of interpreters which sets out why and when to use interpreters, and who these should be.

WEST MIDLANDS PROBATION SERVICE
In March 1995 the West Midlands Probation Service held a conference for and about interpreters in the probation service: 'The first of its kind in the country, the purpose of the conference was to acknowledge, celebrate and share views and to discuss issues of good and bad practice' (from the conference report). The conference addressed a wide range of topics: recruitment, selection, induction, training, shared work, accountability, confidentiality, standard-setting, supervision, support, complaints and administration. Participants discussed training needs both for the interpreters and for probation staff in working with interpreters, as well as how best to meet the requirements of National Standards.

This initiative reflects the expanding use which the West Midlands Probation Service is making of interpreter services, and its awareness of the importance of ensuring that its services will made be available to people in the West Midlands, based on the premise that '. . . access to justice is an essential precursor to the experience of justice'. In common with other probation services, it has a number of bilingual staff. In early 1996, plans for making the best use of these staff, not all of whom are qualified probation officers, were developed. Among other things, the service was keen to ensure that bilingual staff are not exploited or taken advantage of.

Sessional (ie freelance) interpreters are used across the whole range of work covered by the West Midlands Probation Service. There is a substantial list of names, held centrally, but as happens in most public services, only some of those listed are used on a regular basis. At least two colleges in the West Midlands region include in their programme a course leading to the Institute of Linguists' Certificate or Diploma in Public Service Interpreting. This is the preferred qualification required of interpreters by the West Midlands Probation Service. The long-term objective is for all interpreters to be qualified in this way.

The service has developed a formal letter of contract and a Code of Practice for interpreters. The question of access to interpreters has received serious consideration. Amongst the issues which have been identified are:

- how does a client of the service know that there is interpreter provision?
- how is that provision accessed by the client?
- what procedures are in place for a client who requires an interpreter if the need has not been acknowledged by an officer?
- what are the criteria for identifying needs?
- who should be the interpreter?

By far the greatest demand for interpreters in this, as in many other probation areas, is in the Family Court Welfare Service. A leaflet outlining the work of this service is in the process of being translated into a variety of languages explaining:

- what the Family Court Welfare Service does
- the procedures for preparing a welfare report
- how to make a complaint.

The leaflet also urges the reader: 'If English is not the first language of you or your children, please let us know and an independent interpreter will be provided.' As all probation services are now required to spend a proportion of their budget on partnership with other agencies, especially the voluntary or non-profit making sector, the West Midlands Probation Service is considering placing the development of the interpreter service on the 'partnership' agenda. The success of this will depend on securing matching funding and finding an appropriate partner. The expectation is that such a plan, if it succeeds, will have implications for guaranteeing consistent standards of interpreting service for the future.

Members of the West Midlands Probation Service are conscious of the fact that, whilst they have already made some progress towards establishing an efficient interpreter service, there is still a great deal to do:

> We are on a journey of discovery and, whilst we are not necessarily doing it properly, we hope that we are making some progress and will continue to improve. (Probation officer)

A July 1995 report to a county strategy meeting refers to a wide range of issues raised by the Interpreters Steering Group. Topics under discussion have ranged over items such as the use of computer software to enable the probation service to produce PSRs in the offender's first language, and the possibility of including the interpreters service on the partnership agenda.

The group recommends changing its title to the 'Interpreters Service Development Group' in order to make its operation consistent with other parts of the probation service. The purpose of such a group would be to oversee and monitor the use of interpreters and to develop their work. Amongst the many recommendations for consideration in the future are the following:

- the development of interpreter standards of practice, an appraisal framework and a policy regarding professional qualifications
- the development of practice guidelines for work with interpreters
- initiating training arrangements
- the establishment of a complaints system
- identification of targets for divisional use of interpreters based on an assessment of need
- support of interpreters
- examination of partnership and collaboration arrangements
- management of an annual conference.

The report acknowledges the valuable work done by interpreters and the service's resolve to work with them 'productively, positively and professionally'.

Further information about the work of the probation service can be found in *Introduction to the Probation Service* by Anthony Osler (Waterside Press, 1995).

CHAPTER 6

Prisons

The prison population of England and Wales includes a significant proportion of non-English speakers and deaf people who are on remand awaiting trial or deportation, serving sentences, or appealing against a decision of the Home Office concerning deportation. Despite various initiatives to deal with the issue of communication with non-English speakers (see below), the prison service is generally poorly equipped for this.

On arrival at a prison a prisoner or detainee goes through 'reception' procedures, which include answering a questionnaire. This covers a range of topics, starting with personal details and including:

* religion
* immigration
* record of convictions
* court appearances
* informing an embassy
* medical problems
* diet
* languages.

In addition, the prisoner is provided with a Prisoner Information Pack (see below), and with information about property; prison wing allocation; prison facilities; rules and regulations; whom to ask for advice; appeal procedures; entitlements in relation to letters, visits and telephone calls; medical treatment; work; education; adjudications; reports; deportation appeals; refugee status; representations to the Home Office. Finally, there are diagrams illustrating such items as wing routines; a guide for inmates; information about purchases; and a note of some useful phrases. The prisoner or detainee is also seen by the prison medical officer.

The Royal Commission on Criminal Justice (1993) made several recommendations which are relevant in the context of prisons and interpreting:

* the prison service should ensure that prisoners are not taken away from the court precincts before a cell visit by counsel and their instructing solicitor
* during a cell visit, clients should be advised in writing as well as orally

- prison governors should be given adequate resources to enable them to provide interpreters for prisoners who do not speak English so that they can communicate with their lawyers.

To assist non-English speakers, the questionnaire mentioned above has been translated into various languages. However, this still leaves a communication problem for processing officers if no member of staff speaks or recognises the prisoner's language. Additionally, there is the problem of dealing with detainees for whom no translated version of the questionnaire is available. Foreign nationals – particularly those who experienced persecution or torture in their home country – may arrive in a state of confusion and fear (see pp61-62).

A refugee may arrive here having been tortured by the regime in his country and, on seeing the prison, will assume that he is going to be tortured here as well. I have known people barricade themselves in the cell because of this fear. (Prison officer)

For whatever reason, the provision of interpreters appears to have always been a low priority in the prison service. This is likely to continue for the foreseeable future because prison governors are required to meet the costs of all services from their budgets, although it is to be hoped that initiatives introduced before the 1996 cost-cutting round will continue.

In addition to the formal procedures carried out at reception, other features of the prison regime affect a prisoner's ability to communicate effectively and can have an adverse effect on his or her situation. There is also the obvious daily interaction with other prisoners and officers:

There were two prisoners on hunger strike and the situation was becoming very serious. Eventually it was decided that interpreters had to be brought in. It turned out that one of the men was not eating because he thought he would have to pay for his meals and he had no money; the other was just miserable because there was nobody to talk to. (Prison officer)

We tend to get by with a mixture of signs and 'pidgin English' – we do the best we can. (Prison officer)

When I came here I knew no English. Now I speak 'inmate English'. What I thought was a serious thing I would find was a joke; it was very difficult. (Prisoner)

Problems such as these tend to arise mainly in prisons which rarely hold non-English speakers. Where there is a significant number of foreign nationals, interpreting services, translations and support groups are more likely to be provided. Education programmes for non-English speakers are useful but they

132

are mainly arranged for long-term prisoners. It seems that remand prisoners or those awaiting deportation have fewer services.

INITIATIVES

Prisoner Information Pack
The Prisoner Information Pack (1993) issued on reception (see above) is available in several languages. It is a requirement that all prisoners have their rights and obligations explained to them and in particular are advised of the requirements of the Prison Rules. What is unclear, however, is how these obligations are met by prison officers when a non-English speaker or deaf person cannot actually read this information (even in translated form).

Foreign Prisoner Resource Pack
This includes a 'Prisoners' Section' and a 'Staff Section' and was produced jointly by the Prison Reform Trust and the prison service to be used in conjunction with the Prisoner Information Pack. The resource pack is divided into subject areas which are of particular concern to foreign nationals and has been translated into twelve languages. The pack has been revised to make it more accessible to prisoners: the original edition required a relatively high level of literacy skills.

Translations
The Directorate of Inmate Administration holds publications other than the ones described above which have also been translated into languages other than English. These are available to prison staff to use in connection with their work for non-English prisoners. They include 'How to make a request or a complaint'; a 'Race Relations Policy Statement'; and 'Custody, Care and Justice: The Way Ahead for the Prison Service in England and Wales'. Languages into which many of these documents have been translated include Arabic, Bengali, Cantonese, Dutch, French, Greek, Gujerati, Hindi, Punjabi, Spanish, Turkish, Urdu, Vietnamese and Welsh.

Telephone interpreting
A submission to the Royal Commission on Criminal Justice (1993) suggested giving consideration to the establishment of a properly regulated telephone interpreting service for use by statutory agencies. Although only a linguistic form of 'first aid', this type of interpreting can be of considerable use in emergency situations and where distance makes it impractical to have an interpreter come to the non-English speaker's location. In Australia high standards have been achieved by an official telephone interpreting service, which also provides interpreters for 'live' court and other assignments.

133

In addition to using state-of-the art technology, care is needed to ensure that telephone interpreters are not used in inappropriate situations, eg when it is vital to have visual and other contact between the various participants, or in an otherwise complex or delicate communication situation (see Chapter 1). Because of the absence of the visual and personal element, errors can occur more readily in telephone interpreting, and the service provider should take precautions to check that messages have been correctly understood in both directions. Regardless of interpreter calibre, mistakes are always a possibility. The anonymity of telephone interpreters may also make it more difficult to carry out any independent checks and controls of interpreter quality (see Chapter 7, *Professional Standards*).

Where no interpreter is available in Britain – for example, in the case of a rare language – the interpreter providing a service over the telephone may be located abroad. This possibility should be borne in mind, as specifically British expressions, or references to local circumstances, may not be properly understood by the interpreter in question.

Language Line
In 1993 an HM Prison Service notice to staff outlined the trial use of the telephone interpreting service known as 'Language Line'. The introduction to the notice announced the facility in the following terms:

- Language Line available for use in all establishments
- formal three-months trial
- governors to decide whether to use facility locally and, if so, to select staff users and publicise local arrangements
- entry fee costs met centrally by the Directorate of Inmate Administration; usage costs at £1.50 per minute for budgeting locally
- training video to follow.

This document outlined the background to the decision to go ahead with this trial. It referred to the recent increase in the numbers of non-English speaking prisoners, particularly foreign nationals:

As a result demand has grown within establishments for immediate access to appropriate interpreters. Interpreters may not always be available, and it is not always appropriate to use staff or other prisoners with language abilities . . . The facility provides immediate access to interpreters for those working with non-English speaking prisoners.

The document continues with an explanation of the service provided by Language Line and refers to its use by other criminal justice agencies. The cost of running the trial was met by the Directorate but the document made it clear that subsequent use of Language Line would have to come out of individual prisons' existing budgets for non-medical outside staff fees. It also stated:

> [The Directorate] appreciates that existing funding for interpreters is limited; however, Language Line may prove a cheaper alternative to interpretation costs already incurred.

It appears that, at the time of writing, the use of this service has been curtailed at some prisons, for cost reasons.

Using prisoners as interpreters

Traditionally, prisons have improvised, using an inmate who speaks some English to interpret for a fellow prisoner of whose language the 'interpreter' has some knowledge. This questionable practice has a number of potential drawbacks, including insufficient knowledge of one or both languages, inadequate interpreting skills, failure to protect prisoner privacy and confidentiality, and putting one inmate in a situation of power over another. Telephone interpreting provided by a skilled anonymous interpreter, while less than ideal, is certainly preferable to the alternative of 'interpreting' by another prisoner. The same points may apply, in varying degrees, to interpreting by prison staff.

Commitment to improving service to foreign nationals

In 1994, a conference was held by race relations liaison officers working with prisons. The conference report illustrates the commitment of many of the people working in the prison service to improving the level of service to foreign nationals. Questions which were considered included:

- What steps can be taken to improve the identification and recording of foreign nationals on reception?
- What measures can be adopted to reduce foreign nationals' fears during the reception and induction process?
- What practical and realistic action can be taken to make staff aware of the particular needs of foreign nationals?

The conference members produced suggestions to answer these questions, such as the use of cards in a range of languages; inmate interpreters; police and/or customs liaison; making sure the inmate has access to legal advice and the assistance of an interpreter for this purpose; identifying main language and supplying written information in the prisoner's own language; use of outside agencies; contacting students from local institutes of higher education; religious contacts and the use of visiting ministers; effective staff training; and increasing the number of prison officers from minority groups who speak languages other than English.

Initiatives for non-English speaking prisoners

Many innovative schemes are being developed in the prison service by organizations such as the Red Cross (translated medical information), the Prison Reform Trust and others, including volunteers.

An example is an initiative at HM Prison Canterbury, which at any one time has a substantial number of Asian and African inmates, many of whom have a literacy problem. An audio-cassette has been produced with the input of prisoners, interpreters, staff and other interested parties to provide information for non-English speakers who cannot read translated documents. In 1995, one of the staff won an award for his work in developing information for non-English speaking prisoners.

Hopefully, the communication problems of deaf people in prison will receive similar attention in the future, and interpreter provision for non-English speakers and deaf people will become an integral part of prison life.

Deportees

Some further information about foreign nationals who are detained pending immigration procedures and their outcome can be found in Chapter 3.

CHAPTER 7

Professional Standards

Throughout the world, arrangements for interpreting services for public agencies vary widely. At the same time, more and more codes, guidelines and lists of standards are being produced about managing interpreting situations and the performance of the interpreter's role. Each document tends to reflect the outlook of the individual organization which has drawn it up. The issuing body may be a national or regional association of interpreters and translators, or a grouping of people specialising in a particular field, such as legal, medical or sign-language interpreters. Documents may be issued by the body which uses interpreter services with the aim of obtaining uniform practice from freelance interpreters (also known as contract, self-employed, outside, sessional, occasional, *ad hoc, per diem*, and casual or casually employed interpreters); or they may be drawn up by an interpreting organization or project whose goal is to enable non-English speakers or deaf clients to obtain the best possible quality from public-service agencies. They may also include guidance to people who work with and through interpreters; make recommendations and indicate options; and refer to the issuing body's disciplinary arrangements (including sanctions), if any.

In this chapter, examples of best practice have been extracted from handbooks for interpreters, user guides, standards of professional conduct and responsibility, and codes of ethics and good practice in the field of public-service interpreting. The documents originate in a number of countries, including Australia, Britain, Canada and the United States. They apply to spoken language interpreters, sign-language interpreters and interpreters for the deafblind (see Chapter 1, p20). Some are specific to interpreting and legal processes. Others come from associations dealing with interpreters for the public services generally.

Attitudes to a specific issue sometimes vary widely from one set of standards to another. Some codes frankly acknowledge the variable nature of situations likely to confront interpreters. Others seek to lay down rules in a cut-and-dried fashion. Some documents contain explanations, and a considerable amount of detail. Some organizations have disciplinary bodies, to which complaints about failures to comply with their standards can be referred. Other associations have no such procedures, making the provisions of their codes no more than persuasive. Most of the provisions of the codes or guidelines relate, naturally, to the performance of interpreters, but some also refer to the behaviour of other people in the communication process. This makes it clear that quality is a 'two-way street': it can be affected by other people's

137

contributions. It is important to recognise this. Good practice is not the exclusive responsibility of the interpreter.

The following outline is broken down into categories found in some or all of the codes examined by the authors of this work and which correspond to issues affecting interpreters in the legal process. Within the headings, comparative extracts appear from different codes. The only alterations that have been made are those needed to present the extracts in a consistent format.

I. SCOPE AND APPLICABILITY

The following material defines the standards expected by public services of interpreters admitted to the [name of specific register].

II. NATURE OF INTERPRETING

(a) The broad view – to aid communication: The interpreter's job is to interpret everything which the defendant, judge, attorneys and others present would understand if no language barrier existed.

(b) The facilitator, with the interpreter acting as a medium of communication: The primary aim of the interpreter should be to facilitate communication between two persons or groups of persons.

(c) The professional view, with an emphasis on the complexities of the communication situation, in which the interpreter is one of three parties in an exchange: The task of interpreting is complex. It is a professional activity which involves an understanding of the important issues in communication. It brings together three persons of very different interests and backgrounds. It is associated with a large number of variables. This code is an attempt to focus the attention of the interpreter towards the major concerns in such activity.

(d) The translation machine, or the conduit: An interpreter's duty is to translate accurately and precisely the words of a witness from his or her own language into English and the questions to him or her from English into his or her own language.

III. JUSTIFICATION OF HIGH STANDARDS

The client's entitlement to quality interpreting: Interpreters must be competent and fluent: A deafblind person has the right to the best kind of interpreter possible.

IV. QUALITY STANDARDS AND GOOD PRACTICE

(a) Specific instructions: In police and court interpreting, accuracy is particularly important; the interpreter must adhere as faithfully as possible to the original and not add anything or edit anything out, however nonsensical or irrelevant it might appear. He or she should ask for clarification if there is anything they do not understand.

(b) The reasoned approach: The task of interpreting will require that the interpreter should provide a service which aims to be accurate and competent. This is a professional activity and it is important that the interpreter should be sensitive to the circumstances of the interview.

(c) The general communicative goal: To interpret and to translate with the greatest fidelity and accuracy the interpreter can command, endeavouring at all times to communicate the impression of the original.

Interpreters shall interpret truly and faithfully to the best of their ability between the parties without anything being added or omitted.

(d) The linguistic standard to be achieved: Court interpreters shall faithfully and accurately reproduce in the target language the closest natural equivalent of the source language message, primarily in terms of meaning, and secondarily in terms of style, without embellishment, omission or explanation.

(e) The complete approach: Interpreters must provide accurate interpretation of what is said, without embellishments, omissions or editing (ie including epithets). Witnesses are to be informed before proceedings that testimony will be interpreted in its totality. Interpreters must never hesitate to provide the most accurate form of words in spite of a possible vulgar meaning or sexual connotation.

(f) Style and the interpreter as a mouthpiece: The interpreter should use the appropriate 'register' – ie simple or formal language as appropriate, trying to reflect the person's way of speaking as accurately as possible. Even if someone uses obscene or abusive language, this has to be translated into an equivalent term in the other language if the record is to be correct, whatever the interpreter's personal inhibitions – he or she must remember that they are just a 'mouthpiece' and must set aside any embarrassment they might feel.

(g) The complete view – and exceptions: To interpret fully and faithfully what is said, without adding, omitting and changing anything; in exceptional circumstances a summary may be requested and consented to by both parties.

(h) The faithful conveyor of content and spirit (interpreting for deaf people): The interpretation must be faithful to the subject content and spirit of the speaker, the mood of the situation, and visual, tonal and background information.

(i) Fidelity to both the spirit and the letter: The interpreter shall perform his or her work accurately, completely, and clearly with the greatest possible fidelity to the spirit and letter of the original communication.

(j) The verbatim view, idioms and clarification: The interpretation should be as close to verbatim and literal in content and meaning as possible. When idioms or other terms are used that are not co-definitional and the speaker's intent is clear to the interpreter, then the closest appropriate term or phrase should be used. If a term or phrase can reasonably have more than one meaning, or if the interpreter is unfamiliar with the term or phrase, he or she should inform the court of this fact. With the court's permission, the interpreter may enquire further from the speaker to determine an exact meaning. This should occur very infrequently, if the interpreter has had time to prepare for the case.

(k) True meaning and how to achieve it: Interpreters shall endeavour to the best of their ability to translate and interpret accurately by ensuring that the true meaning of words, concepts, statements and bodily expressions is conveyed to the client. This task will be achieved if the interpreter has a grasp of both languages, is aware of the intricacies related to emotional content, strength or force of words, grammatical construction, the double meanings of specific words in certain languages and is consistent in his or her translation of the common meaning of words.

V. COMPETENCE, MONITORING AND EVALUATION

(a) **The desired standard:** Interpreters are required to provide a high standard of interpretation at all times. The interpreter shall interpret to the best of his or her ability in all communications in both directions.

(b) **When accepting engagements:** Interpreters should only undertake engagements which they are competent to accomplish in a satisfactory way.

140

(c) Expectations of interpreters: Interpreters are expected:

- to have written and spoken command of both languages, including any specialist terminology, current idioms and dialects
- to understand the relevant procedures of the particular discipline in which they are working
- to maintain and develop their written and spoken command of English and the other language
- to be familiar with the cultural backgrounds of both parties.

(d) Expertise, professional standards and critical self-evaluation: Instances may arise where knowledge of special terminology is needed in a particular case, or the interpreter may be required to understand uncommon dialects or regionalisms. These instances may cause an otherwise qualified interpreter to be unsuitable for that particular case. Should these conditions arise, and if the interpreter has not been given sufficient information or time to study terminology ahead of time, then it is the interpreter's responsibility to critically assess his or her own ability to perform, and to disqualify himself or herself if not fully capable of providing high-quality interpretation.

(e) Refusing work: It is unprofessional for interpreters to attempt work which they know to be beyond their capabilities. Some police and court interpreting can present particular difficulties and it is perfectly legitimate for an interpreter to say that he or she does not feel competent for an assignment, either beforehand or once they have started interpreting.

(f) Monitoring performance: Good practice will require the evaluation of the interpreter's skill and accuracy.

(g) The dangers of clarification: The interpreter should bear in mind that lengthy conversations with a witness can lead to suspicion and distrust of the interpreter.

(h) Specific interpreting situations: Rules for interpreting for defendant at counsel's table:

1. Speak only loud enough to be heard by the defendant and counsel.
2. Use simultaneous [ie whispered interpreting or *chuchotage:* p19] when the witness is speaking in a language other than that of the defendant.
3. At the defendant's request, and thereafter only by stipulation among counsel, and with the consent of the court, the interpreter may use summary interpretation only:

(a) to inform the defendant of the nature of general procedural discussions between the court and counsel;

(b) for complicated and lengthy testimony by an expert witness if a summary will inform the defendant of the meaning of such testimony more clearly and more expeditiously than simultaneous interpretation.

(i) Skills – The vital elements of interpreting performance: An interpreter should only practise where he or she has sufficient skill, experience and competence.

(j) The specific nature of accreditation: An interpreter should only provide interpretation in languages for which he or she is accredited.

VI. ETHICAL ISSUES

(a) Impartiality: The same general rules of conduct which apply to interpreting for the police [see, generally, Chapter 2] also apply to court interpreting: interpreters should remain impartial and unbiased, should not discuss the case with anyone or disclose any confidential information and should refrain from offering advice, assistance or personal opinions.

(b) Confidentiality: The interpreter should not disclose information to outside parties. It goes without saying that anything the interpreter hears in the course of the interpreting work is confidential and must not be disclosed to any outside parties.

(c) Definitions:

1. Everything interpreted and all conversation overheard between counsel and client is confidential and is not to be revealed.
2. The interpreter should not discuss a case pending before the court.

   - Interpreters undertake to respect confidentiality at *all* times.
   - Interpreters undertake to maintain professional discretion.
   - Interpreters undertake to keep all assignment-related information confidential; not to publicly discuss, report on or offer opinion on a matter in which they are or have been engaged (even if the matter is not privileged); not to discuss any aspects of a case in which they are working with parties, witnesses or jurors.

(d) 'Delegated privilege':Under the Texas Court Interpreter's Act (PL 95-539) the interpreter may not be used as a witness to anything that was said between counsel and client, whether interpreted or not. The interpreter must keep confidential all conversations overheard or interpreted between counsel and client.

Interpreters undertake to protect from unauthorised disclosure all privileged or other confidential information that they obtain during the course of their professional duties.

Interpreters must not make any use of confidential information, including privileged communications between attorney and client.

(e) Privileged/confidential information not to be disclosed:
Before providing professional services, interpreters must disclose on record any services they have previously provided to any party involved in the matter, etc. This disclosure should not include privileged or confidential information.

(f) Conflicts of interest: Interpreters are obliged to disclose all actual conflicts or appearances of conflicts.

The court should be informed whenever the interpreter and any witness are previously acquainted.

Interpreters must disclose if the interviewee or immediate family is known or related to the interpreter.

Interpreters must disclose any business, financial, family or other interest which they might have in the matter being handled.

Interpreters must disclose any information, including any criminal record, which may make them unsuitable in any particular case.

(g) Definitions: Conflict may exist:

1. If the interpreter is acquainted with any party
2. If the interpreter has in any way an interest in the outcome of the case
3. If the interpreter is perceived as not being independent of the adversary parties (or related agencies in criminal cases).

(h) Potential role conflicts: The official interpreter who has been called to interpret at the police station may also be used to interpret for the private consultation between a detained person and his or her legal representative. This should not present official interpreters with any 'conflicts of interest' as long as the interpreter remembers that the consultation is private and that they must not divulge anything that was said. An interpreter does not need to keep a written record.

Interpreters are acting as officers of the court and need to be aware of the importance of maintaining, and being seen to maintain, independence from both parties. For this reason, interpreters must not enter into any communication with the non-English speaker, his or her representative, witnesses, the presenting officer etc, before and after hearings except in the course of their official duties.

Interpreters shall not publicly discuss, report, or offer an opinion concerning a matter in which they are or have been engaged, even when that information is not privileged or required by law to be confidential.

A court interpreter should not render opinions or make subjective statements of any kind through or in connection with a newspaper, radio or other public medium regarding any legal matter in which the interpreter has interpreted or served as a translator of written material of a legal nature.

VII. CONDUCT

(a) Punctuality: Interpreters must appear on time and report to the clerk or designated official.

Interpreters must show reliability.

(b) Dress and behaviour: Appropriate behaviour is expected of interpreters.

Interpreters should wear appropriate clothing for court and be well groomed.

Interpreters must comply with the code of behaviour and formalities prescribed by the specific setting of the assignment (eg court, police).

Interpreters should dress and conduct themselves in a manner consistent with the dignity of the court.

High standards of conduct must be observed.

Rules of professional conduct must be observed.

(c) Gender issues: In personal injury cases, medical cases or rape cases that involve testimony that may be socially embarrassing to a male non-English speaking person with a female interpreter, or conversely, a female non-English speaking person with a male interpreter, this should be made known to the court or to counsel, as it may affect the content of the testimony given, and measures should be taken to put the said person at ease. Ideally, the interpreter is 'sexless', but in reality, this issue sometimes presents a serious stumbling block.

(d) Detachment and rapport: Interpreters must maintain a professional relationship with non-English speaking persons needing services. While rapport built on compassion and understanding should be established, every effort should be made to avoid personal dependency on the interpreter.

The interpreter should strive for a professionally detached relationship. Displays of emotion by the interpreter should be avoided.

The interpreter and the non-English speaker should refrain from addressing one another on a first name basis. Familiar forms such as the *tu* form in French should be avoided.

The interpreter should strive for professional detachment. Displays of emotion, bias or personal opinion should definitely be avoided.

Interpreters should strive to be unobtrusive.

VIII. WORKING CONDITIONS

(a) Modes or techniques of interpretation:

Simultaneous verbatim Simultaneous interpretations shall be executed by a team of two interpreters who shall alternate every 30 minutes or so. This mode of interpretation is very exhausting, and accuracy, speed and concentration cannot be physically sustained for more than 45 minutes at a time. Thus, over the years, the team approach has been found to be the only viable method.

Until such time as simultaneous interpreting equipment becomes available in the courts, this mode of interpretation will have to be executed in a low voice, so as not to interfere with the hearing of others.

Consecutive verbatim This mode signifies a sequential communication of statements or sentences from one language to another. The successive nature of the consecutive mode does not preclude a verbatim interpretation. This mode is the best, and the least confusing way of interpreting for a non-English speaking person who must participate in a dialogue or cross-examination.

(b) Environmental conditions:

The interpreter should endeavour to ensure that the best environmental conditions are available for the execution of his or her duties.

Interpreters should report obstacles to compliance with the rules.

The interpreter has a right to interpreter breaks plus meal breaks.

IX. PERFORMANCE OF ASSIGNMENT

(a) Before the court appearance:
Wherever possible, the appointed court interpreter should interview the non-English speaking witness prior to the initial court appearance.

Non-English speaking persons should be informed prior to the proceedings that their testimony will be interpreted in full, even when they say something obviously not meant for interpretation, the point being that if the said person spoke only English, the remark would have been understood or not made.

Witnesses should be informed before proceedings that testimony will be interpreted in its totality.

Interpreters must obtain the approval of counsel before attempting contact with a witness. Before interpreting begins:

1. The interpreter should briefly familiarise himself or herself with the speech patterns of the witness.
2. The interpreter should determine whether any technical vocabulary is to be used during the testimony (ie the witness's oral evidence).
3. To avoid later confusion, the interpreter may wish to establish a method by which he or she can unobtrusively interrupt lengthy testimony if necessary, eg by using hand gestures. During cross-examination, should a very lengthy question or answer arise, the interpreter may request that it be broken down into reasonable segments to allow a verbatim interpretation.
4. The witness should be advised of the procedure to be followed and acquainted with the interpreter's technique.
5. The witness should be instructed to maintain eye contact with the judge or counsel, but not with the interpreter.
6. The witness should be warned not to initiate any independent dialogue with the interpreter but to direct all statements to the court or counsel.

(b) As proceedings begin: The interpreter shall provide his or her correct name, when requested, for the court record, as well as the language to be interpreted.

The interpreter should strive to enhance the communication process among all parties by providing information and guidance regarding the communication needs involved in the interaction.

The witness' name should be spelled exactly as stated by the witness for the benefit of those in attendance, particularly the court reporter.

(c) During proceedings: The interpreter is responsible only for enabling others to communicate, and is therefore not to take a primary role in such communication; he or she may take a secondary role only as necessary for ensuring an accurate and faithful interpretation.

The interpreter should use direct speech, first person as appropriate.

Always use direct speech . . . The police officer should use the same form, eg 'Were you walking down the road?' and not (to the interpreter) 'Ask him if he was walking down the road.'

146

The interpretation should be conducted in the first and second person, as if the interpreter did not exist. The non-English speaking client should be informed of this, so as to avoid confusion. For instance, the question should be 'What is your name?' *Not* 'Ask him what his name is.' Likewise, the interpreter shall respond for the client 'My name is . . .'. *Not* 'He says his name is . . .'.

The interpreter should be prepared to give clarification of language use if specifically asked to do so by the user or client.

The interpreter should stop the witness or questioner at the end of each sentence and interpret sentence by sentence.

Proper names should not be interpreted but left in their original language.

The interpreter should not emulate the gestures made by the witness.

The interpreter should not emulate the gestures made by the speaker – they have already been seen – emulating the tone of voice is sufficient.

Physical motions express different meanings in each language.

The interpreter shall, at all times, emulate the inflections and intonations of the speaker, in order to reinforce the meaning and stresses of the speaker's words.

During cross-examination, the interpreter should speak in a loud, clear voice, so that he or she may be properly heard in the whole room.

The interpreter should speak slowly and clearly – the adjudicator will usually wish to write down every word said.

The interpreter should spell out any foreign name or place said by the witness.

(d) Interpreting quality: A court interpreter who at any time during a given case feels unable to provide adequate interpretation should immediately address the judge to that effect.

If counsel or the court use a term or phrase which the interpreter believes may confuse the non-English speaking witness, the interpreter must inform the court. These instances may arise when a particular concept is unknown in the witness' native culture or certain English terms are ambiguous in translation (eg, 'you' can be either a singular or plural referent in many foreign languages).

The interpreter should not use an English expression or idiom which is not an exact translation of the witness's own words.

Should the interpreter find at some point in the testimony that he or she has made an inadvertent mistake which was not immediately noticed (ie, in the case of two meanings for a given word: the interpreter chose one and subsequently found that it should have been the other), he or she shall immediately advise the court or counsel that the interpreter made an error and that he or she wishes to correct it.

The interpreter should disclose any difficulties encountered with dialects or technical terms, and if these cannot be satisfactorily remedied, withdraw from the assignment.

If the interpreter has any difficulty in interpreting, he or she must inform the adjudicator immediately – if the interpreter has forgotten the right word he or she should say so, but must not use a word which may give the wrong impression.

(e) The lawyer's responsibilities: If a serious communication problem arises between interpreter and defendant, the interpreter should bring the matter to the immediate attention of defence counsel, who then may request that the court allows time to resolve such problems.

(f) The interpreter's responsibilities: Should a serious communication problem arise between the interpreter and the non-English speaking person, the interpreter should bring this to the immediate attention of the court or counsel, and then may request time to resolve the problems or ask to be replaced.

(g) Deterioration in interpreting quality: If the interpreter believes that the quality of his or her interpretation is faltering due, for example, to fatigue or illness, the court should be so informed.

If the interpreter should become ill or fatigued, he or she shall so inform the parties involved.

(h) If asked to sight-translate technical documents: The translation of highly technical documents is not part of an interpreter's duties. If asked at court to provide an 'instant' translation of such a document, the interpreter is quite justified in saying that unless given adequate time and without proper preparation any translation can at best be provisional.

(i) Impartiality: To avoid the appearance of prejudice, the interpreter should avoid unnecessary discussions with counsel, parties, criminal defendants, witnesses or other interested parties inside or outside the courtroom.

(j) General information: The interpreter may give general information to the non-English speaking person regarding the time, place and nature of court proceedings. In matters requiring legal judgement, the individual must be told to obtain legal advice.

k) Leaving: An interpreter should not leave the courtroom until proceedings are officially terminated or until he or she has been officially excused.

After the hearing the interpreter may still be needed to help the defendant or witness understand any course of action to be taken as a result of the hearing, and he or she should not therefore leave until sure of being no longer required.

The person who interprets at court (ie for the defendant) should not normally be the same person who interpreted at the police station. The police station interpreter is, at least potentially, a prosecution witness and may be asked to attend court as a witness and possibly give evidence about the previous interpreting work.

X. THINGS THAT AN INTERPRETER SHOULD NOT DO

(a) Interpreters should not:

- give legal advice
- act as an advocate
- counsel, advise, influence or offer personal opinions
- take personal advantage of any information obtained in the course of their work
- provide opinions to public media
- act as a legal officer or consumer
- undertake responsibilities outside their area of competence as an interpreter
- allow personal opinion to influence the performance of their work
- discriminate against parties, either directly or indirectly, on the grounds of race, colour, ethnic origin, age, nationality, religion, gender or disability
- speak to a witness before or during a hearing except in the course of their official duties
- correct an erroneous fact or statement that may occur in a question posed to the non-English speaking person, even though the error is obviously unintentional or simply a slip of the tongue: likewise, the interpreter should not correct an obvious error in the testimony of a non-English speaking person. Neither should the interpreter infer a response, that is, if the non-English speaking person is asked to clarify a prior response, the interpreter should pose the question as asked and not volunteer what he or she thought the person meant.

(b) Interpreters engaged by the police: Interpreters should not be left on their own to obtain statements from victims or witnesses. The police officer is responsible for the content of the statement and the interpreter merely acts as a channel of communication, so must always work under a police officer's guidance.

Similarly, interpreters should never go to a victim's or a witness's home to take a statement on their own; the interpreter must be accompanied by a police officer.

The interpreter should never be left on their own with a prisoner; the police officer and/or solicitor must be present at all times.

It is not the interpreter's responsibility to produce a summary of an interview.

XI. EMPLOYMENT/BUSINESS TERMS

(a) The assignment: Interpreters must accurately and completely represent their pertinent testing credentials, training, and experience.

All interpreters are required to complete and sign an application form as to what languages they can speak, read and write.

Interpreters have a right to refuse assignments without a reason.

The interpreter should, without prejudice, decline work if he or she believes it to be beyond his or her technical knowledge of the subject involved, his or her linguistic capacity or accreditation.

Interpreters should not accept work which they know to be beyond their competence linguistically. In circumstances where a more suitable interpreter is not available an interpreter may accept such an assignment providing that both the user and the contractor are informed of the legal and service implications.

(b) Conditions of employment/assignment: Interpreters should not accept favours and gratuities of any kind.

The rule is 'Do not accept gifts'.

Direct sole payment should be made by the employer.

(c) Fees: Interpreters should not accept less than fees set by [name of national institute of interpreters and translators].

Interpreters should maintain a fair and reasonable schedule of fees in civil cases, particularly if referred to clients by the court.

Interpreters should request remuneration in a professional manner.

A *per diem* interpreter (ie a contract interpreter: see the *Glossary*) should maintain accurate and detailed time records of services rendered.

(d) Financial status: Interpreters must not provide services if remuneration is contingent on the outcome of the case.

Where employed by a public agency, an interpreter must not solicit private work from clients of that agency.

(e) Liability and insurance: The interpreter will be liable if he or she provides a service which is inaccurate or incompetent, or he or she commits a breach of confidentiality. It is recommended that an agency which supplies an interpreter should make arrangements for insuring against such shortcomings.

XII. PROFESSIONAL DEVELOPMENT

Education and training: Interpreters should:

- engage in continuing ongoing education
- engage in further training
- constantly improve their skills
- strive to enhance their professionalism
- engage in self-education.

Interpreters are responsible for engaging in continuing education to keep themselves informed of matters which can improve their performance; should be responsible for elevating the standards of performance of the interpreting profession and should seek to maintain a professional relationship with all court officers and legal personnel; should develop a compendium of standard phraseology for handling interpretation of proceedings such as administering of rights, oaths, the *voir dire* and standard judicial admonishments; should demonstrate professional solidarity with colleagues (mutual assistance).

XIII. DISCIPLINARY PROCEDURES AND SANCTIONS

(a) Complaints procedure: Interpreters should be fully conversant with [any relevant] complaints procedure.

(b) Disciplinary procedures: Violation of interpreting codes may lead to removal of the interpreter from [name of register].

The organization's disciplinary body has absolute discretion to determine the meaning and apply the provisions of [the relevant] code, and its decisions will not be subject to appeal. Where the complaint is upheld, the disciplinary body may admonish, suspend or exclude the interpreter from the register.

Court interpreters shall abide by the rules of professional conduct of [the relevant organization]. An accredited court interpreter who violates these rules is subject to removal from the register.

CHAPTER 8

Beyond England and Wales

This chapter charts developments in certain other countries and provides examples of good practice outside England and Wales in the provision of interpreters to work in the legal system.

Rights and good practice
On the whole, enlightened countries now accept the need to ensure that interpreters are provided for people who do not speak or understand the language of criminal proceedings in which they are involved. Documents such as the European Convention for the Protection of Human Rights and Fundamental Freedoms (see pp75-76) or the International Covenant on Civil and Political Rights stipulate that individuals who are arrested must be informed in a language which they understand why they have been arrested and what they are charged with; must be enabled to defend themselves, including examining witnesses; and must be provided with an interpreter without charge to themselves.

Unless the interpreting provided under these requirements is accurate and of good quality (see, particularly, Chapters 7 and 9), however, these are hollow rights. In England, the principle laid down in these and other human rights documents was recognised as early as 1916 in *R v Lee Kun*: yet it is only 80 years later – as the millennium approaches – that the need to ensure that competent interpreters are employed in the criminal justice process is at last beginning to be addressed.

Similarly, it was many years before the authorities in the USA finally recognised the unfairness of trying someone who has no understanding of English without providing an interpreter. In the wake of *Negron v New York* (1970) and pressure from the civil rights movement, the Court Interpreters Act of 1978 was passed. This acknowledges the need to provide interpreters for people who require foreign-language or sign-language assistance in legal proceedings in the federal courts. Ten years later, further legislation requiring the provision of *competent* interpreting services acknowledged the vital aspect of quality. It also recommended the simultaneous rather than the consecutive mode of interpretation (see pp18-19). At first, certification for interpreters was offered only in the Spanish-English combination, which covers 92 per cent of cases requiring interpretation in the US federal courts.

In Canada, section 14 of the Charter of Rights and Freedoms guarantees the right to an interpreter in legal proceedings. When the Canadian Supreme Court examined interpreting issues in *R v Tran* (1994), it ruled that in order for the language-disadvantaged person's presence in court to be meaningful, the standard of interpretation must be high. For Canadian judges, this meant that the interpretation must be continuous, precise, impartial, competent, and contemporaneous. The European Court of Justice has similarly made a start in acknowledging the importance of quality in interpreting (*Kamasinski v Austria* (1989)).

In the southern hemisphere, acknowledgment of Australia's multicultural population led in the 1980s and 1990s to major improvements in arrangements for the provision of interpreters in legal proceedings in that country. Certification, university-level training and registers, together with the organization of proper interpreting services, improved standards considerably.

In an increasingly mobile world, with crises in a particular country triggering refugee flows to various other states, interpreting needs can fluctuate widely. It is unrealistic to believe that certified interpreters will be available in all countries for all language combinations in all legal settings. A country's traditional attitudes to education, training and languages affect its approach to the issue of interpreting provision in public services, including the legal system. Tradition similarly affects a country's approach to language rights and the technicalities or practicalities of legal proceedings. Regardless of the specific arrangements in any given country, however, the outcome should be the same: no one should be involved in legal proceedings in a language which they do not understand or speak sufficiently well unless they are provided with competent interpreting services at all stages.

Technology and quality control

The human element continues to play a vital role in the provision of interpreting services. Nevertheless, technology has considerably expanded traditional interpreting options. 'Electronic' simultaneous interpreting (see pp18-19), which enabled the multilingual post-WWII Nuremberg war crimes tribunals to take place, can be extremely useful for multi-defendant trials. It speeds up hearings and its use is routine in all the proceedings of the European Court of Justice in Luxembourg, as well as in Canada's Supreme Court. In California, for trials involving several defendants, each non-English speaker was previously entitled by law to his or her own interpreter. The resulting cacophony can be imagined. A change in legislation made it legally possible for a single interpreter to work into a given language, and technology enabled any number of defendants to listen to that one interpreted version.

Telephone interpreting, using conference-call technology, can provide a stop-gap solution for short, urgent procedures, or before an interpreter arrives. This technique can, for example, enable non-English speaking prisoners in high-security prisons to consult with their legal advisors. Because of the absence of the visual element, audio phones cannot be used effectively for most two-way interpreting situations or, quite obviously, for the deaf.

In 1995, remote interpreting, using video-conferencing techniques, was introduced in Singapore for some civil cases and small claims tribunals. Such technical developments make it possible to make more effective use of interpreter resources. Subject to safeguards, they might also make it possible to provide sign-language interpretation from a distance.

Concerns about the quality of interpreting – basically accuracy and completeness – sometimes surface specifically in connection with the use of technology. These should always be addressed even where a system has built-in 'quality control'. In Japan, a restricted form of simultaneous interpreting was introduced in the mid-1990s. Interpreters, provided with advance copies of written submissions in Japanese, gave a simultaneous rendering to which the non-Japanese defendant listened through headphones. Some lawyers worried about the absence of any check on what the interpreter was saying using the simultaneous technique. Through an electronic discussion group on the Internet, a Japanese researcher asked about other countries' quality assurance arrangements for interpreting in legal situations. Overwhelmingly, the answer was, basically, 'nothing'. An experienced Spanish-English interpreter gave the following picture of his experiences in the USA:

Checking the accuracy of interpretation is also a problem in the US Courts. They usually go by whether the answers to questions are responsive. Defendants may complain if they cannot understand the interpreter. When translation issues come up on appeal, the court only has an English record to go on. In those circumstances, the court will bend over backwards to find "harmless error".

The principal "guarantee" of accurate translation is certification of the interpreter. Unfortunately, there is no certification exam for most languages. Even in Spanish, the certification process is completely inadequate.

Even in civil cases, sometimes with millions of dollars at stake, law firms often find themselves without competent interpreters. Checking the accuracy of an interpretation is not really that hard. It is simply a matter of always recording the foreign language portion of proceedings. There are machines that will produce many hours of recordings on an ordinary audiocassette. Recorders are used for all sorts of frivolous purposes, but not to record foreign language spoken in court.

I got into the habit of carrying a microcassette recorder with me in court. Especially at the stand, with the judge's permission, I would record the Spanish of the witness and my translation, in case of challenge, or even for my own peace of mind. (Private correspondence)

154

Good practice round the world

Some countries try harder than others in the difficult but vital area of legal interpreting. Introduced by a list of issues and variations in relation to public-service interpreting (based on a planning guide for designing a training programme for community interpreters drawn up by Bruce Downing and Laurie Swabey of the University of Minnesota), there follow below several 'snapshots' of good practice in countries beyond England and Wales.

- Accreditation
- Authorisation
- Availability – Who interprets? What qualifications do they have? Is there a certifying agency? If so, who is certified? How are interpreting services organized (staff interpreters, freelance, public referral service, commercial agencies)? Within a community, are there qualified interpreters or bilingual people who might become qualified interpreters?
- Certification
- Conditions of employing interpreters – including contractual obligations, cancellation charges, insurance, provision of documentation, briefings, manning strengths
- Costs – of providing interpreting services, training interpreters, of wasted court time in the absence of competent interpreting services
- Enhancing interpreters' skills and knowledge – development and training
- Fees to interpreters for various assignments and conditions
- Funding (for training, for courses, for services)
- Goals – eg 'equal access and equitable treatment for non-English speakers and cultural minorities'
- Increasing service providers' cultural sensitivity
- Interpreter educators (trainers) – are they available for the appropriate language pairs? Can they be found to do the training? Are they trained as educators? Have they trained interpreters?
- Legal entitlements and requirements for interpretation services
- Legal status of the interpreter's words (the 'hearsay v agency' argument: according to the agency viewpoint, the interpreter's words must necessarily be equated with those of the language-handicapped user because that particular interpreter has been chosen and hence adopted as 'agent' by that user. The interpreter's words can thus be considered to be those of the speaker and, therefore, can be reported by any individual who did not understand the original utterance without hearsay occurring. The 'hearsay' argument maintains that only the interpreter can testify as to what was said by the foreign-language speaker: the evidence of anybody who heard the interpreter's version and testifies on that basis would be hearsay and hence *prima facie* inadmissible).

- 'Manning' strengths – how many interpreters to be engaged for long or complex assignments for what language combinations?
- Market: in which languages are public services available, which public services require interpreters, what legal mandates are there for interpreter services? Must interpreters be provided? Qualified? Certified? Are these mandates enforced? How are interlingual service encounters currently managed?
- Monitoring of performance
- Needs – how many, which languages, which dialects, continuing influx, future projects?
- Police officers as interpreters – principle, calibre, performance, dangers, advantages
- Profession – is court/legal/judicial interpreting seen as one?
- Programmes and programme types – which are needed/possible/desirable? Academic/certificate/undergraduate or post-graduate/community college, etc; course sequence? private instructional programme?; in-house staff training, introductory workshops, continuing education?
- Qualifications
- Quality control, quality assurance
- Recruitment of trainees
- Registers of interpreters
- Skills needed by interpreters
- Statute, case law, charter, requirement, recommendation, best practice
- Statutory requirements to use certified/authorised/official interpreter?
- Teaching and training materials – audio, video and printed
- Technology – use of interpreting booths, use of wired or wireless equipment, legal implications
- Techniques – consecutive (with or without note-taking), simultaneous (out loud, whispered, or 'electronic' from booth), summary
- Training programmes for community interpreters – are any available? In what form, what quality? (eg by agencies, language classes only, training in specialised terminologies only, workshops). Where are programmes located, what do they cost? What languages are included in programmes, what interpreting skills/specialities do they prepare students for?
- Training programmes for selected bilingual/bicultural individuals to develop cross-cultural communication and interpreting skills; and for service providers to work more effectively with interpreters
- Training the trainers
- Transcribing
- Translations: from translating in-house, to referrals to competent translators, to teaching service providers how to write texts so that they can be more readily translated

156

- Word lists, glossaries, etc – terminology
- Working conditions – number of interpreters, breaks, provision of documents, briefing sessions, monitoring arrangements.

The provision of interpreting services
It is instructive to consider a few specific examples of developments in the provision of interpreting services beyond England and Wales:

AUSTRALIA
With the introduction of a multicultural Australia policy, the provision of quality language services was recognised as a vital element in an overall co-ordinated strategy to redress the multiple disadvantages caused by language and cultural barriers that migrants from non-English speaking backgrounds had historically faced in their contacts with public and other services. In the 1980s, the expansion and enhancement of the quality of legal interpreter services were identified as a major priority.

In Australia, testing of and accreditation for both translators and interpreters are carried out by the National Accreditation Authority for Translators and Interpreters (NAATI), established in 1977.

VICTORIAN INTERPRETING AND TRANSLATING SERVICE (VITS)
An example of language services in Australia is the Victorian Interpreting and Translating Service (VITS), a state-owned company which came into being in January 1991 as a result of the consolidation of the Victorian Government's Language Services within the Office of Ethnic Affairs. It incorporates specialist services in the areas of legal, mental health, education and conference interpreting, a translation service, an ethnic communication consultancy and marketing.

The service's human resources consist of a group of highly skilled 'core' personnel together with access to over 800 contract interpreters and translators, accredited at professional and advanced professional level.

State-of-the-art technology enables telephone interpreting to be provided on a 24-hour, seven day a week basis. An automated dialling system provides access to qualified, accredited interpreters within a maximum of two minutes of identifying the language required.

Set up in 1984, the specialist Legal Interpreting Service (LIS) is accessible all year round, day and night. All of its interpreters hold a minimum of NAATI Professional Level accreditation. In addition, they are required to have completed the specialist Legal Interpreter Orientation Course. This is designed to enhance knowledge of the legal system, legal terminology, court procedures and interpreting techniques in the legal setting. In the decade following the service's establishment, it put on 25 such courses, each lasting for 40 hours. More than 500 interpreters covering 64 languages were recruited by LIS.

In consultation with user departments in the legal area, LIS has produced glossaries of legal terms in twelve languages. These provide a precise, consistent list of terms which may be encountered in a broad range of legal and quasi-legal situations. This is of particular value in circumstances where a clear understanding of difficult legal terms and concepts is essential to the process of communication and consequently to the achievement of justice. The glossaries have been well received and accepted by both the interpreting profession and the legal establishment.

The Legal Interpreter Orientation Course is designed to provide interpreters with a basic knowledge of the structure and functioning of the state's legal system and of other departments serviced by LIS. It also aims to ensure that interpreters have a clear and precise understanding of their role as interpreters in the legal system, including their legal status. Issues such as professional ethics and interpreting techniques are constantly reinforced. Appropriate simulation exercises are designed to focus on the effective interpretation of legal terminology. The theoretical components are transferred into a practical exercise at a 'mock hearing', where interpreters have the opportunity to apply their enhanced knowledge of court procedures and interpreting techniques in a courtroom setting.

Aware of the need not only to provide a quality service, but also to ensure that appropriate *use* is made of that service, every year VITS runs an average of 100 seminars on 'working with interpreters'. Through these endeavours, it seeks to raise the awareness of a broad range of professionals in the public sector, such as police, social workers, lawyers, magistrates and administrators, as to the appropriate use of interpreters, in order to facilitate better communication with non-English speaking clients. VITS activities with interpreters and user agencies have helped to dispel attitudinal misconceptions about the need for and role of an interpreter, and to engender a heightened sense of professionalism.

ONTARIO, CANADA

The London Cultural Interpretation Service, Ontario, reflects a view of interpreting which goes further than a purely linguistic framework. It acknowledges the need to address cultural issues, and sees the interpreter as a cultural as well as a linguistic mediator. As the service's documentation explains, the following issues must be addressed in situations requiring proper communication between English-speaking service providers and non-English speaking clients:

1. Linguistic competence

2. Accurate information
3. Impartiality
4. Confidentiality
5. Cultural bridging
6. Professionalism
7. Liability
8. Training
9. Convenience
10. Reasonable fees.

The service facilitates access to 100 trained cultural interpreters, covering 40 different languages and dialects. The role of the cultural interpreters is defined as helping service providers to understand the culture of their clients. The interpreter can interpret 'the messages, values and assumptions hidden behind the words'. In this way, he or she can prevent misunderstandings arising from cultural differences or stereotypes. The services provided by Ontario's cultural interpreters cover:

- on-site interpretation, including confirming the appointment with the non-English speaker
- conference calls (three parties – service provider, non-English speaker, interpreter – at three different locations)
- information relay: the interpreter obtains and relays information between the client organization and the non-English speaker at different times, usually by telephone. Most often used to arrange an appointment, transmit brief instructions, or deliver a message. Includes communicating response or confirming receipt of information
- training programmes for selected bilingual/bicultural individuals to develop cross-cultural communication and interpreting skills; and for service providers to work more effectively with interpreters
- translation of written texts.

A non-profit organization, the service is partially funded by the Ontario Ministry of Citizenship. Its freelance interpreters are covered by 'errors and omissions insurance'.

Legislation
The following 1995 text from Victoria illustrates legislative awareness of the fact that when the police have to question people who do not understand English well, a *good* interpreter must be engaged in order to ensure that proper communication takes place, and that this is a *right*, not a concession to the non-English speaker:

Section 464D. *Right to an interpreter*
(1) If a person in custody does not have a knowledge of the English
language that is sufficient to enable the person to understand the
questioning, an investigating officer must, before any questioning or
investigation under section 464A(2), arrange for the presence of a
competent interpreter and defer the questioning or investigation until the
interpreter is present. (Source: *Victorian Statutes*, July 1995 release, Crimes
Act 1958: Part III – Procedure and Punishment, Division I – Pleading
Procedure, Proof, Etc: (30A) – Custody and Investigation)

Training

Attitudes to training interpreters to work in community (ie public service)
settings vary widely, as the following examples illustrate.

SWEDEN
Developments in Sweden disclose a particularly interesting hybrid approach
which combines adult education and university input. Community interpreting
is provided for over 150 languages. It is estimated that there are more than
5,000 interpreters working in Sweden, of whom only a small proportion are
authorised. Community interpreter training courses are arranged in order to
provide the interpreters to whom immigrants are entitled in their contacts with
government agencies, including the courts, as well as other services such as
social welfare departments, hospitals, or employment exchanges.

Stockholm University's Institute for Interpretation and Translation Studies
(IITS) has overall responsibility for the training of community interpreters in
Sweden. The shortage of teachers qualified to teach many of the immigrant
languages at university level means that most of the training courses for
community interpreters take place in an adult education setting, as does the
training of interpreter trainers.

Training courses for community interpreters consist of a number of
separate subject units (each requiring 80 hours of study). An introductory course
is followed by units on interpreting for the social services and social insurance
offices, medical interpreting, general legal interpreting, and interpreting for the
labour market and workplace needs. Each course involves studying the relevant
social institutions, the ethics and techniques of interpreting, and training in
interpreting and terminology in both Swedish and the other working language.
Advanced courses for a specialised qualification are also given in court
interpreting and medical interpreting. Additional short courses address such areas
as the specific techniques and ethical considerations involved in interpreting for
children.

Training programmes for interpreters at Swedish adult education institutes
('folk high schools') are often organized on a weekend or one-week residential
basis. At adult educational associations, trainees may attend for a few hours a

160

week over a longer period of time. Basic interpreter training programmes at universities require one academic year of full-time study (40 weeks or 320 hours). The state provides a considerable amount of funding for interpreting training, whether on an institutional or a personal level. Thus trainees receive free board and lodging during their course, as well as some degree of compensation for loss of income and travel expenses. Students on university courses can apply for government study loans. Tuition is always free of charge.

An alternative route is for students to take the basic course in interpreting at Stockholm University's IITS. While the university's course units differ from the vocational courses at adult education centres, they always cover the same basic areas. There are also courses in Swedish and the other working language, including factual knowledge about relevant countries and cultures. The final examination is on the same level of difficulty as that taken by trainees who have followed the adult education route.

Authorisation of interpreters is granted by a national judicial board on the basis of testing. Interpreters who have successfully completed the one-year basic interpreting course at a university are exempted from sitting the board's tests, but are still evaluated for suitability as community interpreters.

IITS produces teaching material for various courses, with the help of external experts. To date it has also produced word lists for interpreters in 17 languages. The institute also supplies recommended syllabuses for the community interpreter training programmes run by adult educational institutions.

CALIFORNIA, USA

In a totally different approach in California, the Monterey Institute of International Studies (MIIS) runs a variety of Spanish-English court interpreting courses. These include courses to improve Spanish and English skills; a four-week intensive introduction to court interpreting (130 hours of instruction); intermediate court interpreting (two weeks, 65 hours); preparation for written examinations for court interpreters (one week, 30 hours); and a one-week 26-hour advanced court interpreting course, for students who have already passed the California written exam for court interpreters and are preparing to take the California oral examination.

BRITISH COLUMBIA, CANADA

The following material, taken from the prospectus for the Court Interpreting Certificate Programme of Vancouver Community College and Langara College – Continuing Education Division, reflects a view of court interpreting as a profession for highly educated individuals with linguistic and other skills. The Vancouver course is designed accordingly:

Court interpreting . . . requires superior linguistic skills – but they alone are not sufficient. A professional interpreter needs to be knowledgeable of, and skillful in using, a variety of interpreting techniques as they relate to his or her specific job. In addition, the court interpreter has to have a sound knowledge of the legal system, as well as an awareness of the procedures and terminologies used in the courts. He or she must also be able to communicate effectively with all parties involved in legal proceedings, and act according to accepted rule and order.

The Vancouver courses are scheduled in the evenings and on occasional weekends: over the September-May academic year, students' activities include 195 hours of class instruction and internship. The Court Interpreting Certificate is recognised as proof of accreditation by the Ministry of the Attorney General, Court Services (British Columbia). Courses include:

1. Orientation to interpreting – presentation of interpretation as a process of interlingual communication, and of different modes of interpretation. Seminars in professional development, terminology research and storage, code of ethics, public speaking.
2. Bilingual interpreting – practice of sight translation and consecutive interpretation using legal and other texts in sessions for each language of speciality. Introduction to simultaneous interpretation. Interpreting practice in mock trials and other simulated or community interpreting situations. Court observation and reporting.
3. Law for court interpreters – discussion of legal aspects of court interpreting, and the role of the interpreter in the legal system. Introduction to the Canadian and British Columbian court system, and principles of law. Court procedures and terminologies.

In order to be accepted on to the programme, applicants must have an excellent command of both English and another language, written and oral; post-secondary education; good hearing; and an aptitude for interpreting.

Training materials
In addition to offering courses, another approach to training is for official agencies to provide written material. An example is the range of freelance court interpreters' handbooks issued by the Court Interpretation and Translation Services of the Ministry of the Attorney General in Ottawa, Ontario. Apart from giving rules of professional conduct and guidelines on avoiding bias, this extensive training material includes detailed handbooks covering:

- courtroom procedure
- interpretation techniques

162

- the justice system in Ontario
- criminal procedure (basic concepts, first steps in criminal procedure, the trial and decision, summary of criminal procedure, criminal law glossary)
- common offences (impaired driving, offences against rights of property, offences against the person, breach of court orders, drugs and narcotics offences)
- provincial offences court
- family law matters (including a family law glossary)
- civil actions (including a civil law glossary)
- small claims court
- constituent elements of the criminal code
- compilation of charges.

Questions appear at the end of all chapters except for the one on interpretation techniques, which contains a series of exercises. By way of illustration, outlines appear below of the contents of the two training chapters on shoplifting and sexual assault. Similar packages have been prepared for proceedings relating to traffic offences, impaired driving, drugs and family law.

Shoplifting
The training chapter is designed to familiarise court interpreters with the legislation which governs theft, the typical characteristics of shoplifters, the vocabulary used in such cases, the kind of witnesses to expect and the type of testimony they might give, defences which might be put forward and the common range of sentences which might be imposed by the judge. Exercises throughout this chapter test interpreters' knowledge and help to sharpen skills. The chapter contains the following material:

- Shoplifting – An overview of the problem
- Offences against rights of property
- Informations
- The shoplifter
- Short answer questions
- Some shoplifting lore
- Store security and the police
- Breach of trust
- The guilty plea
- Police reports
- The shoplifting trial
- Sentencing
- Probation order
- The stop-lifter programme

- Conclusion
- Shoplifting crossword puzzle
- Fill-in-the-blanks exercises
- Just for fun (limericks)
- Appendix A – Offences against rights of property – Sections 321-378 of the Criminal Code
- Appendix B – Articles on shoplifters
- Appendix C – Transcripts of trial proceedings
- Appendix D – Newspaper articles on shoplifting and related offences
- Appendix E – Answers to exercises
- Appendix F – Shoplifting lexicon (English-French).

Sexual assault
The materials here comprise:

- Part I: Introduction, child abuse, incest, legislation pertaining to offences of a sexual nature, the interpreter's role, evidence which may be presented, expert witnesses, child witnesses, exclusion of the public, exclusion of witnesses, order of non-publication, questions on the victim's sex life, late disclosure of a sexual assault
- Part II: Sections of the Criminal Code pertaining to offences of a sexual nature (English and French texts). Sample of wording found on an information relating to a sexual assault charge: English and French examples
- Part III: Glossary
- Part IV: Sample reports, etc: psychological consultation note; psycho-sexological evaluation; sexual assault history forms; evidence; pre-sentence report (French and English)
- Part V: Interpretation exercises (English) (newspaper reports and other articles)
- Part VI: Interpretation exercises (French) (newspaper reports and other articles)
- Part VII: English-French lexicon: terms related to sexual assault matters
- Part VIII: English-French lexicon: sexual terms related to sexual assault and those relating to prostitution
- Part IX: Medical terminology – English-French lexicon (contents: lexicon; root words; prefixes; suffixes; human skeleton; human anatomy)
- Part X: Transcript of a preliminary enquiry in a sexual assault case
- Fill-in-the-blanks exercises.

Conclusion

In the modern world, interpreting is just as delicate and challenging an activity as ever. Technology has increased options for its provision, but its inherent difficulties still remain. The professionalism and skill of the individual interpreter is the main factor in determining the quality of the service provided. The quality of justice is inevitably compromised if interpretation does not meet the same high standards as those of the entire system. The examples cited above illustrate a variety of approaches to the training of interpreters and users, as well as to the provision of interpreting in legal settings. There is no one 'right' model. It is impossible to achieve perfection across the board for all languages and all situations. Nevertheless, essential factors can be identified as being a concerned and resourceful approach to interpreting, as well as adequate funding of training and interpreter provision.

Some interpreter services see their role as going beyond simply engaging people to provide a linguistic link in given situations. Thus they may also put on activities to enhance user awareness of communications and cross-cultural issues, and to train people in how best to use interpreting and translating services. They may also assume responsibilities for producing glossaries and training materials.

The aim of all such activities is to raise standards and thereby improve the quality of language services provided in the public services. Such good practice contrasts with many authorities' traditional laissez-faire attitudes to interpreting. Regardless of whether an interpreter in court (or elsewhere in the legal process) is a professional, that interpreter should perform competently.

ADDRESSES

London Cultural Interpretation Service
200 Queens Avenue, Suite 510
London, Ontario
N6A 1J3
Canada
Tel: (519) 642 7247
Fax: (519) 642 1831
Email: lcis@info.london.on.ca

Ministry of the Attorney General
Court Interpretation and Translation Services
161 Elgin Street, Suite 5200
Ottawa, Ontario
Canada
Tel: (613) 239 1335
Fax: (613) 239 1460

Monterey Institute of International Studies (MIIS)
Translation and Interpretation Division
425 Van Buren Street
Monterey CA 93940
USA
Tel: (408) 647 4170
Fax: (408) 647 4199

Stockholm University
Institute for Interpretation and Translation Studies (IITS)
S-106 91 Stockholm
Sweden
Tel: (08) 16 20 00
Fax: (08) 16 13 96

University of Minnesota
Program in Translation and Interpretation
190 Klaeber Court
320 16th Avenue SE
Minneapolis MN 55455
USA
Tel: (612) 624 4055
Fax: (612) 624 4579

Vancouver Community College
Court Interpreting Program
Continuing Education Division
100 West 49th Avenue
Vancouver, BC V5Y 2Z6
Canada
Tel: (604) 323 5322

Victorian Interpreting and Translating Service (VITS)
1st Floor, 371 Spencer Street,
Melbourne 3000
Australia
Tel: (03) 9280 1955

CHAPTER 9

Wind-Up

At the beginning of Chapter 4, *Interpreters and the Courts,* several questions were posed but left unanswered. The information contained in this book gives (or implies) answers to those questions. Much remains to be done, however, before acceptably high standards of interpreter services are finally achieved across the legal system. No one person or group can – or should – be expected to assume sole responsibility for attaining these standards. This concluding chapter expands on some of the major issues.

Standards of interpreting

Interpreting standards could be raised for everyone involved in the legal process if relevant matters were to be addressed by each person affected by them. In the current atmosphere of partnership and 'working together', it should be possible to achieve this. Although there are many examples of good practice scattered around the United Kingdom, information about such initiatives is not filtering through. For example, a suggestion that interpreter representatives be included in the membership of court user groups – whose purpose is to promote better understanding, cooperation and coordination in the administration of criminal justice – has been welcomed in some areas. One such example of good practice is the Uxbridge Magistrates' Court User Group, which not only includes an interpreter in its membership but at the time of writing is preparing a *Best Practice Guide* on a wide range of matters to include issues regarding the use of interpreter services. Unfortunately this enlightened approach is far from widespread and is even viewed with suspicion by some people.

A nationwide survey of court users (including defendants and witnesses) carried out for the Royal Commission on Criminal Justice (1993) did not include interpreters or non-English speaking defendants and witnesses in its scope. This regrettable omission might not have occurred if there had been a greater awareness of interpreting issues.

Awareness of issues

In a BBC television programme (*Panorama,* 10 July 1995), issues closely related to the subject matter of this book were spotlighted. The programme looked at the predicament of a number of British citizens who had fallen foul of the authorities in certain European countries. An English building worker arrested in Germany on a relatively minor charge complained that he had been remanded in custody because, in his opinion, as a foreigner, he did not have the same access to bail as local residents. In Portugal, two British men accused of attempting to murder a German found it hard to follow the court proceedings against them. There was no reference to providing English-language interpreting services so that they could do so. The German-Portuguese interpreter who relayed the testimony of the victim was shown searching for the German word for 'moustache', the implication being that she was not providing a high-quality, accurate version of what was being said – the main evidence against the English-speaking defendants.

The message of the *Panorama* programme was that other countries' legal systems are different from our own, and that Britons abroad should not expect to encounter British standards of justice elsewhere. Language issues were not the main focus of the programme, but the message was clear: apart from a defence lawyer who, hopefully, will speak some English, do not expect the other people with whom you will come into contact to speak English, nor even to communicate with you through an interpreter. And if you have dealings with an interpreter, do not expect that person to be competent. The British national who comes into contact with a European criminal justice system is likely to be isolated linguistically and culturally. For many viewers, this message must have been disturbing. Yet many European countries could probably make similar programmes about the experiences of their nationals abroad in any other European Union country – including Britain. The unfamiliar and probably incomprehensible legal system; the difficulty of obtaining bail as a non-resident; the language barrier; the problem of obtaining competent interpreters – all these factors apply just as forcibly to non-Britons in this country as they do to the British abroad. Indeed. one of the few differences will probably be that an English-speaker abroad will have a better chance of finding a lawyer who speaks some English than a non-English speaker in Britain will have of finding a lawyer who speaks his or her own language.

It is hard for people brought up and educated in the English language in Britain to grasp the frustrations experienced by people from a different background when facing a justice system which is literally foreign to them. The *Panorama* programme went some way towards conveying the feelings of frustration and despair of people (in this case, from England) who come into contact with an alien criminal justice system. It is not just the language, but also the very nature of the system that they do not understand. The difficulties that confront them in dealing with the system are more than linguistic, but the language factor is the most obvious one.

Interpreter competence
The legal system should provide competent interpreters wherever necessary to assist with the communication process at all stages. This will then offset the disadvantage suffered by individuals who are not fluent in spoken English (nor to a lesser extent in written English either) whenever they come into contact

168

with the law. Using interpreters in an efficient and effective way can save time and money, and can be a factor in reducing stress for all parties to a dispute.

Current practices concerning the engaging of interpreters to work in English courts suffer from several major handicaps. Many of those responsible for running the system have little or no grasp of what is involved in interpreting and consequently they do not understand what is needed. Even when somebody has realised that communication problems do exist in a particular case, there may be practical difficulties about obtaining the services of a competent interpreter. Often the administrative staff responsible for engaging interpreters have little real experience in this field. As this book went to press, a debate was underway as to the basic matter of *who* (prosecution, defence or courts) should have the responsibility for 'warning' an interpreter for a court appearance (*New Law Journal*, 5/19 July 1996).

As a British government spokesman has acknowledged, 'in a perfect world one would wish to find the services of qualified interpreters available all the way down the scale' (Lord Renton, House of Lords, *Hansard*, 26 March 1991). The question is thus: in the imperfect world that we all inhabit, to what extent is it acceptable for *unqualified* interpreters to appear in the justice system? In a country which prides itself on its high standards, the interpreters whose words shape the outcome of proceedings should be competent to perform their duties. What is interpreter 'competence' and how is it to be achieved? There are two main aspects to proficiency in this area:

• linguistic and interpreting skills
• knowledge of a particular organization (system) and its procedures.

In order to interpret between two languages ('both ways'), interpreters should have high-level proficiency in both languages. This proficiency may have been acquired naturally (eg growing up in a bilingual household or being educated in a language other than that spoken in the home), or by study. Interpreting skills are usually acquired through formal courses, which often do not include a language component as such. Interpreting courses in this country include a variety of options, such as:

• undergraduate or post-graduate university level courses in conference interpreting, such as those at Bath, Bradford, Heriot-Watt, and Westminster
• university level sign-language interpreting courses, such as those at Bristol and Durham
• courses leading to a specialist qualification, such as the Diploma of Public Service Interpreting (DPSI). This is administered by the Institute

of Linguists and run at a variety of further and higher education establishments
- non-university level training courses for sign-language interpreters, primarily run by organizations such as the Royal National Institute for Deaf People (RNID) and the Council for the Advancement of Communication with Deaf People (CACDP)
- induction courses, such as those run by the London Interpreting Project (LIP).

Some of these courses include specific modules dealing with the legal system, for example the DPSI Legal Option (England and Wales), or the DPSI Legal Option (Scotland).

Whether qualified or not, interpreters need to attend specialised training courses dealing with particular facets of the legal system, either because they should keep up with developments, or because they have not covered in depth aspects of that particular field, such as the criminal courts, police station interviews, interviews with children, sexual abuse, prison interviews or specific tribunals. Even highly experienced and qualified interpreters should have continuing training opportunities made available to them. The issue of funding cannot be ignored here: service providers require financial support so that they can provide in-service training or send their 'official' interpreters to regional courses. The outcome should be cost-effective because interpreting services should improve and savings will be made in the longer run. It should be noted by interpreters that not all courses include a legal option. It can be difficult to locate both academic and vocational training courses within a reasonable travelling distance. There are moves to make some courses fit in with National Vocational Qualifications (NVQs), and it is often worth enquiring at local colleges whether there are any suitable courses available.

Specialised training courses are even more difficult to locate. A few magistrates' courts have devised short introductory courses, and some of the agencies within the legal system (such as the police and social services) put on occasional courses for interpreters. It is essential that there is an expansion of such initiatives. Hopefully, the National Register of Public Service Interpreters, which emerged from the work of the Nuffield Interpreter Project – and which is now administered by the Institute of Linguists – will result in a greater awareness on the part of service providers of the existence and availability of qualified interpreters. The National Register includes information about the languages offered by interpreters, together with their qualifications and the areas in which they work.

Training courses are needed not only for interpreters, but also for practitioners who work through interpreters. There is a skill involved in working efficiently and effectively through interpreters, something not widely recognised. A few such courses have been run in the UK in association with specific courts. Where they have been organized, there has been general acclaim largely because issues have been raised which had not previously been thought about by the participants (magistrates, court clerks, members of the Crown Prosecution Services, court administrators). People who have attended such courses report that as a result they became aware that they have a responsibility to know how to work effectively through interpreters.

Quality assurance and cost-effectiveness

Quality considerations are frequently not addressed when interpreters are engaged. When agencies from outside the formal system are used by officials to recruit interpreters, quality control is often utterly absent. In effect, the system is then 'paying over the odds' for an inexperienced (and possibly incompetent) person who just happens to speak two languages. Direct recruitment does not necessarily give a better result, although at least in this case the employer has more control over the engagement and does not pay a fee to an intermediary.

The payment of fees is controlled to a certain extent by guidelines issued by the relevant authorities, such as the *Guide to Allowances under Part V of the Costs in Criminal Cases (General) Regulations 1986,* issued by the Legal Services Division of the Lord Chancellor's Department (LCD, January 1989 and amended as of 1 March 1996). At para 4.9 this states:

> The amounts allowed to interpreters (including sign-language interpreters) for the accused are at the discretion of the court. This is to allow courts to pay the going rates for interpreters and thus ensure a regular and sufficient supply of people qualified in the necessary languages. The discretion recognises that the availability and expense of obtaining an interpreter in one place will not be the same as in another place. The only exception to the court's discretion is in respect of fees for Welsh Language interpreters in courts in Wales. For these there is a prescribed allowance determined by the Lord Chancellor.

At para 4.11, that document goes on to say:

> Court staff should note that where a witness for a defendant or a private prosecutor requires an interpreter, payment of the interpreter's fees (which are at the discretion of the court) can be made under Regulation 16(1), if the court considers it to be an expense properly incurred by that witness.

The wording of para 4.9 begs the question of what the 'going rates' are. At a local level, some court administrators apply the Lord Chancellor's Department range of fees for interpreters on the basis of languages and related supply and demand considerations. The question is, 'Is it the spirit of natural justice for interpreters of different languages to be paid different rates in the same locality, regardless of their skills?'. Such a simplistic approach ignores relevant criteria such as interpreters' skills, qualifications and experience, and the length and complexity of cases, together with other relevant factors.

Guidelines for payment by the police are issued by the Home Office and by the Association of Chief Police Officers (ACPO). These too can create local variations, as identified in the following extracts from correspondence in the publication of a professional organization (June 1995):

> I am still registered as an interpreter with the . . . police, but recently I turned down an interpreting job, running over three days, for the following reason: the first hour is paid at under £15 and subsequent hours are paid around £7. Take it or leave it. I left it! . . . Since then, I have heard that rates vary considerably between one authority and the next. I would be interested to know of other interpreters' experiences.

In response, the police force in question made the following comments:

> Guidelines received from the Home Office state that the level of fees payable to interpreters is a matter for negotiation and agreement by the appropriate Police Authority. Accordingly, within . . . the current interpreting rates, although considerably lower than those suggested by yourself, have been approved by the appropriate Authority and are to be implemented until their next review in April 1996. I shall take into account your comments when the rates are next calculated (although it is unrealistic to imagine that they will be increased to £35 per hour).

The exact nature of the contractual relationship between interpreters and people who use their services is unclear. This results in inconsistencies in conditions and levels of fees – and ultimately, in a reluctance on the part of professional interpreters to accept engagements for criminal proceedings. There is usually no written contract for an individual assignment, and the terms of an engagement (including cancellation fees) are often utterly unclear.

It is essential that for payment purposes interpreters are not treated as witnesses when they are engaged to interpret at court proceedings. In March 1996, at least one prosecution area was sending out witness payment forms to interpreters instead of appropriate interpreter payment forms. The fees for witnesses are generally lower than for interpreters, and these forms can therefore result in interpreters not being paid at an appropriate level to reflect their status, expertise and skills. Such forms can also give misleading information to interpreters, who may think that they are being appointed as witnesses to some event instead of in a professional, interpreting capacity.

Certain organizations – representing the interests of clients or consumers of current interpreting services – as well as individual lawyers, are becoming increasingly aware of the implications for justice of variable interpreting standards. In 1995, several proceedings involving British Sign Language (BSL) interpreting for deaf defendants were stayed or stood down on grounds including:

- the quality of the interpreting at the police interview
- errors in the interpreting provided during the court proceedings
- the number of interpreters engaged for a particular trial.

Quality control can be achieved in a number of ways, although it is generally accepted that it is a difficult issue to address. Clear criteria are essential for any organization which has responsibility for employing personnel. Such criteria, which should include interpreter competencies, would go some way towards setting standards. The problem is one of identifying whether or not criteria are being met. As things stand, there is often no provision for checking interpreter performance. Practical options for improving standards include:

- engaging several interpreters for the same language combination, to work in turns so as to reduce fatigue and increase accuracy
- monitoring the performance of the interpreter on duty by the off-duty interpreter
- making appropriate use of technology, including microphones and amplification/transmission equipment for interpreters and clients alike
- electronically recording everything said in court, in both languages (original or 'source' language and interpreted or 'target' language)
- making a transcript of everything said in court, in both languages (in the original or 'source' language and interpreted or 'target' language)
- using an additional (independent) interpreter to monitor the performance of the 'official' interpreter
- monitoring by a qualifying body/examining body/inspectorate
- the use of disciplinary panels to deal with complaints.

If such options were available, criticism of an individual interpreter's performance could be dealt with objectively and fairly. An example of such procedures is provided by the National Register of Public Service Interpreters already mentioned (see p170):

[These] are standards expected by public services of interpreters admitted to the National Register. In order to maintain those standards, public services and clients who are dissatisfied with the performance of an interpreter recruited through the Register are requested to supply details to

173

the Institute of Linguists. Any disciplinary action will be decided upon by the disciplinary panel described in section 5 of the code.

Any complaint against an interpreter thought to be acting contrary to this code may be referred by the Institute of Linguists to the National Register Disciplinary Panel. Although not explicitly stated, presumably the proceedings of the panels include an opportunity for the interpreter to explain himself or herself. In the absence of such a structure, unfair or arbitrary action might be taken against individual interpreters. Reports from interpreters who have worked in various parts of the legal process indicate that interpreters can be removed from official lists without being informed of the reason or being given the opportunity to be heard. It would appear that the presumption of innocence and natural justice do not apply here. There is also a contrasting problem, ie where an interpreter whose removal from a list has been ordered by a senior member of the system continues to appear in that system. The result is that interpreters whose performance is not up to standard continue for many years to delay and confuse proceedings.

Service providers and others should keep themselves properly informed of developments, in order to make the best use of initiatives and to avoid misinformation, such as that which appeared in the new version of the Police and Criminal Evidence Act 1984 (PACE) Codes of Practice (10 April 1995). Police officers consulting that version of the Codes for advice on how to obtain interpreters in the mid-1990s read exactly the same advice – much of it by then out of date or misleading – as their predecessors a decade earlier.

The interpreter's place in the 'court team'
The way that things are structured in England and Wales, an interpreter is isolated at work, without colleagues with whom to share problems and interact, and with no professional structure.

Where an 'interpreters' office' exists (at the time of writing, the authors have only come across these outside England), the interpreter is an accepted member of the organization, whether working as an employee or freelance. To know that there is an administrator with a specific responsibility for directing the interpreter to the relevant court, to give guidance and information, and to deal professionally with matters such as recruitment, payment and training, is in stark contrast to the experience that many interpreters have when arriving at an English court: searching for an usher who may or may not know where the interpreter should go; walking into court clutching coat, bag, etc (nowhere to put them); and then at the end of an exhausting day seeking out a hostile administrator, only to find that the fee has to be negotiated and is dependent on the administrator's individual and possibly arbitrary perception of the complexity and length of the interpreter's day. These are two extremes. It is

174

hoped that efforts will be made to eliminate the latter version in favour of a more 'interpreter-friendly' and 'interpreter-aware' working atmosphere.

Service providers, particularly those responsible for writing guidelines for interpreters, should be aware of these issues, and balance helpful information about the nature of the organization and its procedures with the obligations and standards expected of freelance interpreters. An example of good practice in the compiling of guidelines is identified in Chapter 2, *Interpreters and the Police*. The opening message to the South Yorkshire Police *Notes of Guidance for Interpreters and Police Officers* addresses the following request to officers:

> ... Please remember that the interpreters are often professional people with advanced linguistic skills, and they should be treated accordingly.

These *Notes*, in common with many others, provide a good balance of specific and general information for interpreters, as well as for the personnel (professional and administrative) involved with them at various stages of an assignment.

This book does not seek to produce a cut-and-dried definition of the duties and behaviour of interpreters in the legal process. It recognises that interpreters may well have to adapt their approach to suit different settings and specific situations. In some public-service settings, the role of the interpreter may include drawing attention to cultural issues. In other contexts, the definition of the interpreter's role may be so narrow as to exclude all but the linguistic aspects of communication. The problem with this approach, which legal figures often seek to impose, is that language cannot be artificially separated from culture in its broadest sense. At the opposite end of the scale, even within the legal system interpreters are sometimes considered to have duties that go far beyond the role of a linguistic (and perhaps cultural) mediator. Some judges seem to expect them to play an active or investigative role, while certain police guidelines imply that they should carry out not just secretarial, but also editorial duties, such as summarising tapes of police interviews, and lawyers may even try to use interpreters as part-time secretaries and messengers. It cannot be emphasised strongly enough that the interpreter's role does *not* include the duties of secretaries, editors, juniors, messengers or investigators.

The importance of the pre-trial conference

Traditionally, there has been little contact between interpreters and those who work in the courts. There may be no panacea for this situation. However, one recommendation that the authors of this work would like to float is that before a trial begins, a short 'conferencing' session should be held, attended by the main professional 'players' – the judge or the magistrates and their legal advisor, the lawyers and the interpreter(s). At this session interpreting issues would be addressed and procedural matters referred to, in order that agreement can be reached about what behaviour and performance standards are expected of the interpreters, and what they in turn can expect (and ask) of speakers and others involved in the proceedings. Specific issues could be addressed, such as providing interpreters with documents in advance and during proceedings; how interpreter queries are expected to be dealt with if they arise during trial proceedings; interpreting issues related to legal argument; and the judge's explanation to the jury about the interpreter's presence and role.

A conferencing session would result in more efficient communication during a trial and a greater understanding on the part of law practitioners, court personnel and interpreters of their respective roles in the proceedings when a non-English speaking or deaf person appears in court. Such a procedure (which could also be applied with appropriate modifications to other interpreting situations arising out of legal processes) would also enable the system and its members to learn more about interpreting than is often the case at the moment.

Moving forward together

All members of the 'court team' (judges, magistrates, advisors, lawyers, administrators, interpreters, etc) need to move forward together in order to develop a mutual understanding of the role and responsibilities that each member has in striving for higher standards in interpreting. This book has sought to spark awareness of the issues which need to be addressed within such a framework. It is hoped that these will be taken on board in the spirit of the various initiatives, developments and improvements which have been identified in this work. With appropriate adaptation to local conditions, they can be built on and expanded in order to achieve desirable standards.

Epilogue: A Backwards Look Forwards

In 1535 the explorer Jacques Cartier claimed for France the area around the St. Lawrence River in what was to become Canada. There was a clear need for some communication with the native Iroquois Indians if trading links were to be opened and the French position consolidated. To expedite matters Cartier kidnapped two of the Iroquois and took them to France for eight months to learn French. He then brought them back to Canada to act as interpreters. The French expected the two Iroquois interpreters to be loyal to their cause. However, when conflicts of interest arose, the interpreters sided with their fellow Iroquois. Disgusted, the French recaptured the recalcitrant pair and returned them to France, where they died in exile.

• • •

Numerous historical examples illustrate many of the issues and principles that are addressed in today's court interpreting settings. The following extracts shed light on topics that have been mentioned in the preceding chapters, including the provision of interpreting services, the interpreter's role, the ethics of interpreting, quality control, and the impact that the interpreting process has on the bench and the lawyers.

'Borosky': Entitlement to an interpreter

An early illustration of interpreted legal proceedings is found in the seventeenth-century English political murder trial of *Borosky and others (1682)*. The accused were a Polish labourer, two foreign 'gentlemen', and a Swedish count. Between them they spoke French, German, Dutch and English with varying degrees of fluency. The following passage makes it clear that when it came to deciding about who was entitled to an interpreter, class – not linguistic need – was the decisive factor. The person who speaks the best English is the aristocrat – and he gets the best treatment from the court:

Lord Chief Justice: Ask the other, the captain, the same thing.
Sir Nathaniel Johnson (interpreter): He desires a French interpreter, for he speaks French.
Lord Chief Justice: Surely here are enough people that understand French, but ask him if he does not understand English.
Sir Nathaniel Johnson: He can understand some, he says.
Lord Chief Justice: Now then, ask my Lord Coningsmark what he says.
Sir Nathaniel Johnson: He speaks English, my Lord.
Lord Chief Justice: But not well enough, maybe, to understand the whole.

Lord Chief Justice North: Sir Nathaniel, what does he say?

Sir Nathaniel Johnson: My Lord, he says it is a concern of his life, and therefore he desires he may have not one interpreter, but others: he desires he may have two or three, that they may make no mistake.

Lord Chief Justice: Very well.

Sir Nathaniel Johnson: He says . . . I understand the Dutch language; but his life and honour are concerned, and therefore he would have three or four.

In the case of the nobleman, the court accepted the principle that there should be several interpreters who could check on each other's performance and take turns in working. Over 300 years later, attempts by English professional associations of sign-language interpreters to achieve precisely the same working conditions in order to improve quality standards incurred the wrath of the bench in *R v Ragu Shan* (1995).

Advocate, witness or interpreter?

In *Borosky's* case, some of the legal participants, typical of certain educated English circles at the time, spoke a number of languages. This made it possible for them to identify and comment on unprofessional behaviour by the person engaged to provide interpreting services, a certain Sir Nathaniel Johnson:

Lord Chief Justice: Can you speak of his credit, Sir Nathaniel Johnson?

Sir Nathaniel Johnson: Of the merchant's credit I can, my Lord; I know him to be a man of considerable estate and credit. He is a man of such reputation, that he would not send a man of an ill reputation.

Sir Francis Winn: You may observe, my lord, how Sir Nathaniel Johnson – who is interpreter in the case – is a witness, and argues for the prisoner too. My Lord, we desire to take notice of Sir Nathaniel's forwardness; for it may be a precedent in other cases.

Lord Chief Justice: What do you talk of a precedent? When did you see a precedent of a like trial of strangers, that could speak not a word of English; but you would fain have the Court thought hard of, for doing things that are extraordinary in this case.

In this case, the Lord Chief Justice was certainly at fault, in asking the 'interpreter' to contribute material which clearly lay outside the limit of an interpreter's duties. The comment of another member of the court reflects the eternal frustration of the legal profession with unprofessional behaviour by 'interpreters':

Sir Francis Winn: We observe what a sort of interpreter Sir Nathaniel Johnson is: he speaks more like an advocate than an interpreter; he mingles interpreter, and witness, and advocate together, I don't know what to make of him.

In 1682, a multilingual trial of foreigners with interpreters was a rarity in England. This may explain the Lord Chief Justice's inappropriate attitude towards the interpreter, who was certainly no professional. More than three centuries later, such cases have become fairly routine: yet within the legal system, judicial attitudes towards interpreters and those needing interpreting services still vary widely. It is almost as if, every time there is a situation requiring interpreters, the system is taken by surprise and has to improvise.

Queen Caroline and the Bill of Pains and Penalties: Monitoring

In *Borosky*, one of the accused suggested that more accurate interpreting would be provided if a number of interpreters were present, each checking on the performance of the others. This is precisely what happened at the 1820 'trial' of Queen Caroline of England. The estranged spouse of King William IV was accused of having committed adultery during an extended trip abroad. All of the witnesses who gave evidence against her were foreigners and were examined through interpreters.

The interpreter offered by the House of Lords, where the trial (the 'Bill of Pains and Penalties') took place, was an Italian aristocrat, the Marchese di Spineto. He turned out to have been engaged by representatives of the Foreign Office and Treasury. Counsel for the defence considered this a potentially biased arrangement, and at his insistence a second interpreter was sworn in on behalf of the Queen. This meant that there were then two Italian interpreters in court, and so it was possible to carry out quality control of the interpreting. Some of the judges hearing the case also had a limited knowledge of Italian, and they queried various renderings. The following example is one of many interpreting issues in the proceedings:

Question: While you remained at Milan did anybody give you money?
Answer: (witness, in Italian, answering through interpreter): I remember not: I remember that nobody did: I do not know.
Question: What is the answer you mean to give?
Answer: I remember to have received no money when I arrived at Milan; I remember I did not; 'non so': I do not know; 'piu no': more no than yes; 'non mi ricordo': I do not remember.

The interpreter's technique in the above passage makes the translation process visible both to the participants and to later readers. This practice is exceptional, as the record normally contains no trace whatsoever of the words in the original language. However, since the witness's three-part reply ('I remember not; I remember that nobody did; I do not know') appeared to contain unclear and perhaps contradictory statements, their lordships wished – quite rightly – to make sure that they had properly understood it. When the witness was asked to specify which of the three statements he had intended to give, he appears to have expanded upon his original answer. When the interpreter put the witness's second answer into English, this time he repeated some of the original Italian, in order to show that any confusion was present in the *original* and not the result of mistakes in his rendering.

Because of the lingering doubt about the confusion in the English version of the witness's answer, the second interpreter was asked by the court whether he agreed with how the Marchese di Spineto had interpreted the witness's answer. He replied that he did agree with it, making the situation somewhat clearer, but no more satisfactory. 'The Earl of Roseberry said that it was most essential that the House should understand what the meaning of "non mi ricordo" was; whether it was that the witness did not remember a certain event, or that he remembered that no such thing occurred.' In a final effort to clear things up, 'Lord Longford begged that the last answer given by the witness should be repeated to him by the interpreter, from the shorthand writer's notes.' The doubt as to the speaker's real intention remained: but at least the court had done everything it could to ensure that the source of the confusion was not faulty interpreting. Television viewers who followed the USA trial on a murder charge of the film actor O J Simpson (who was acquitted) would have observed that a similar issue arose in the testimony of a Spanish-speaking housekeeper. Across the centuries, the interpreter's predicament has not changed.

Cultural informant

The record of the proceedings against Queen Caroline also shows that the court would ask the interpreters to shed light on cultural issues which were important in order to understand evidence properly. The following example focuses on the precise meaning of an Italian word used by the interpreter when addressing the witness. One of their lordships pointed out that the word 'servants' had been rendered as 'Le Corte', and the interpreter was asked whether that would include the personal attendants on her royal highness:

> *Marchese di Spineto:* "It would include the whole of the establishment of a person of the rank of Her Royal Highness." This was acquiesced in by Mr. Cohen [the second interpreter].

Another example involves food. The interpreter was asked what 'polenta' was. He stated that 'it was like porridge made of maize, and a favourite dish in Italy.' Sometimes the interpreter volunteered information in order to prevent misunderstanding. For example, in the following extract he was aware that the

English participants in the proceedings would not understand the way the Italians told the time:

> *Question:* As nearly as you can recollect, what hour was it you passed through the garden of the Villa d'Este with Domenico Brusa?
> *Witness (through interpreter):* About one or half-past one.
> *Interpreter:* The Italian and the English time is reckoned by a different manner.
> *Question:* Do you reckon by the Italian or the French hour?
> *Witness:* The Italian hour.
> *Interpreter:* We reckon the hour, not from twelve to twelve, but from one to twenty-four; the Sun, according to the Italian mode of calculation, always sets at half an hour past the three and twenty, the remaining half hour is generally allowed for twilight, and that completes the twenty-four hours.
> *Mr. Solicitor to the interpreter:* Will you translate into English time the time?
> *Interpreter:* Then I must know the time of year: taking it at Bartholomew's day, it would be about half-past nine at night, according to the English mode of calculating.

The Solicitor-General observed that he doubted whether the people of Lombardy actually calculated the time by the Italian method, but that it was important to clarify whether the time was half past nine or half past one:

> *Question:* When you say it was about one or half-past one that you saw Pergami and the princess sitting in the manner you have described, according to the best of your recollection, how long was it after sunset?
> *Answer:* The sun had been setting for an hour and a half.
> *Mr. Cohen (second interpreter):* My lords, I was born in Lombardy myself, and I know this is the mode of reckoning.

Strictly speaking, interpreters do not volunteer information on their own initiative: but in this case, not to have drawn the court's attention to the issue would have led to a major misunderstanding. Without the information provided by the two interpreters, the court would have understood that Princess Caroline had been in the garden in broad daylight. Were the interpreters right or wrong in behaving in this way?

• • •

Technological progress has not changed the dilemmas facing the interpreter in the legal system. Nor has the greater frequency of interpreted proceedings in today's legal system brought about an overall change in attitudes. How much, if at all, have judicial attitudes to interpreting services progressed from those illustrated in the seventeenth and early nineteenth century cases quoted above? Are contemporary procedures for engaging interpreters, interpreting quality assurance and quality control arrangements worthy of the standards on which the English justice system traditionally prides itself?

* * *

An Egyptian tomb sculpture dating back some three and a half thousand years shows a 'Siamese twin figure' which some have identified as an interpreter. The two heads, each pointing in opposite directions, can be understood as showing the two-way process of interpreting. Cynics have suggested, rather unfairly, that the interpreter is just being two-faced! Well-documented reports from around the world identify issues which are as relevant today and probably as old as language itself.

Appendix I: Some Useful Addresses

Association of Police and Court Interpreters (APCI)
284 Lewis Trust Buildings, Vanston Place, London SW6 1AW
0171 381 0953

Council for the Advancement of Communication with Deaf People (CACDP)
Pelaw House, School of Education, University of Durham, Durham DH1 1TA

Institute of Linguists (IoL)
24a Highbury Grove, London N5 2DG
0171 359 7445

Institute of Translation and Interpreting (ITI)
377 City Road, London EC1V 1NA
0171 713 7600

London Interpreting Project (LIP)
The Print House, 18 Ashwin Street, London E8 3DL
0171 923 3437

London Open College Federation (LOCF)
15 Angel Gate, City Road, London EC1V 2PT
0171 278 5511

The Association of Court Interpreters and Translators (TACIT)
Flat 4, Cornwall Gardens, London SW7 4BA
0171 937 0616
Email: 100600.2701@compuserve.com

Most of the above organizations hold lists of interpreters.

Appendix II: Cases and Statutes

R v Kingston-upon-Thames Magistrates' Court, ex parte Davey 149 JP 744 (1985)
R v Lee Kun (1916) 11 CrAppR 293
R v Mayor and Burgesses of the London Borough of Tower Hamlets, ex parte Jalika Begum [1991] Imm AR 86
R v Mercier (1777) 1 Leach 183
R v Pritchard (1836) C&P 303
R v Ragu Shan Old Bailey 11 September 1995 (unreported)
R v Rampling Times Law Report August 29 1987
R v Secretary of State for the Home Department, ex parte Assadorn, Court of Appeal (Civil Division), 20 October 1989
R v Secretary of State for the Home Department, ex parte Dhirubhai Gordhanbai Patel [1986] Imm AR 208
R v Secretary of State for the Home Department, ex parte Wu (CO/2078/89), 8 May 1991
R v Sharp [1960] 1 QB 358
R v Steel (1787) 1 Leach, CC 451
R v Thomas Jones (1773) 1 Leach 102
R v Tran [1984] 2 SCR 951
R v Turnbull [1976] 3 All ER 549; [1977] QB 224
R v Van Axel and Wezer, September 1991, Legal Action 12
R v Yscuado (1854) 6 Cox, CC 386
Singh v Singh Court of Appeal, Civil Division [1971] 2 All ER 828
Trepca Mines Limited, Re (1960) 1 WLR 24
United States ex rel Negron v the State of New York 310 FSupp 1304 (1970)
United States v Desist 36 ALR3d 255 (1967)

STATUTES

Statute of Pleading 1362, 36 Edw II, St 1, c15
Concerning the laws to be used in Wales 1535, 27 Hen. VIII, c26
An Act for turning the Books of the Law, and all Process and Proceedings in Courts of Justice, into English, II Acts and Ordinances of the Interregnum (1650)
An Additional Act concerning the proceedings of the Law in English (1651)
Courts of Justice Act 1731, 4 Geo II, c26
12 Geo 3, c20
Criminal Lunatics Act 1800 (39 & 40 Geo 3, c94)
Criminal Law Act 1827, 7 & 8 Geo 4
Welsh Courts Act 1942
Welsh Language Act 1967
Oath Act 1978
Welsh Language Act 1993

Further Reading

Adams, Christine, Corsellis, Ann and Harmer, Anita (eds). 1995. *Basic Handbook for Trainers of Public Service Interpreters*. Nuffield Foundation, London

Berk-Seligson, Susan. 1990. *The Bilingual Courtroom: Court Interpreters in the Judicial Process*. University of Chicago Press, Chicago

Berlins, Marcel and Dyer, Clare 1994. *The Law Machine*. Penguin, London

Brooke, Mr Justice. 1992/1993. 'Ethnic Minorities: Seven Points to Remember', *The Magistrate*, 48:10, 194-195

Butler, Ian, and Noaks, Lesley. 1992. *Silence in Court? A Study of Interpreting in the Courts of England and Wales*. University of Wales College of Cardiff. Commissioned by the Nuffield Interpreter Project

Chandler, David, and Colin, Joan. 1992. 'Training for Court Interpreters: A Local Initiative', *The Magistrate*, May 1992, 66

Colin, Joan. 1993. 'The view from the bench: a case for training', in Picken, C. (ed), Vol. 2, 189-191

Commonwealth Attorney-General's Department. 1991. *Access to Interpreters in the Australian Legal System*. Australian Government Publishing Service, Canberra

Corsellis, Ann. 1995. *Non-English Speakers and the English Legal System: A Handbook in Good Practice for Those Working in the Legal System Across Language and Culture*. University of Cambridge, Institute of Criminology, Cambridge.

de Jongh, Elena M. 1992. *An Introduction to Court Interpreting Theory and Practice*, University Press of America, Lanham, Maryland.

Edwards, Alicia B. 1995. *The Practice of Court Interpreting*. John Benjamins Publishing Company, Amsterdam and Philadelphia

Hatim, Basil and Mason, Ian. 1990. *Discourse and the Translator*. Longman, London and New York.

Jolliffe, Paul. 1995. 'A Code of Practice for Interpreters in the Magistrates' Courts', *The Magistrate* 51:9, 208.

Kyle, J. G. and Woll, B. with Pullen, G. and Maddix F. 1985. *Sign language – The study of deaf people and their language*. Cambridge University Press, Cambridge and New York

Lester, Cathy and Taylor, Veronica. 1994. *Interpreters and the Legal System*. Federation Press, Sydney.

Levi, Judith N., and Walker, Anne Graffam. 1990. *Language in the Judicial Process*. Plenum Press, New York and London.

Mellinkoff, David. 1963. *The Language of the Law*. Little Brown and Company, Boston and Toronto

Moerman, Ellen *et al.* 1993. *Court Interpreting: A Survey of Needs, Services and Problems in Criminal Proceedings*, ms.

Morgan, Diana. 1982. 'The Life of a Court Interpreter', *Graya*, 86, 51-52

Morris, Marshall (ed). 1995. *Translation and the Law*. American Translators Association Series, Vol. VIII. John Benjamins Publishing Company, Amsterdam and Philadelphia

Morris, Ruth. 1993a. 'Justice for non-English speakers - Interpreters and the Legal Profession', *New Law Journal*, 23 July 1993, 1059-1060

Morris, Ruth. 1993b. *Images of the Interpreter: A Study of Language-Switching in the Legal Process*. Unpublished PhD thesis, Department of Law, Lancaster University

Morris, Ruth, 1993c. 'The Interlingual Interpreter – Cypher or Intelligent Participant? Or, The Interpreter's Turn . . .', *International Journal for the Semiotics of Law*, VI/18, pp. 271-291

Morris, Ruth. 1995. 'Pragmatism, Precept and Passions: The Attitudes of English-Language Legal Systems to Non-English Speakers', in Morris, M (ed), 263-280

Niska, Helge. 1995. 'Just Interpreting: Role Conflicts and Discourse Types in Court Interpreting', in Morris, M (ed) 1995, 293-315

O'Barr, William M. 1982. *Linguistic Evidence: Language, Power, and Strategy in the Courtroom*. Academic Press, New York, London, Paris

Picken, C (ed) 1993. *Proceedings, XIIIth World Congress of FIT, Translation – the vital link*. Vols 1 and 2. Institute of Translation and Interpreting, London

Polack, Kenneth, and Corsellis, Ann. 1990. 'Non-English speakers and the criminal justice system', *New Law Journal*, 1634-36 and 1676-77

Roberts, Celia, Davies, Evelyn and Jupp, Tom. 1992. *Language and Discrimination: A Study of Communication in Multi-ethnic Workplaces*. Longman, London and New York

Sacks, Oliver. 1990. *Seeing Voices*. Pan Books, London

Seabrook, Mike. 1992. 'Swearing in Court', *New Law Journal*, 842

Shackman, Jane. 1984. *The Right to be Understood*. National Extension College, Cambridge

Silas, Douglas. 1993. 'Deaf Jurors', *New Law Journal*, 896

Stanley, Alison. 1990. 'Political asylum interviews: the role of clerks and interpreters', *Immigration and Nationality Law and Practice*, 91-93

Tusa, Ann and Tusa, John. 1983. *The Nuremberg Trial*. Macmillan, London

Vassenaix, Anne-Sylvie. 1995. *The Present Situation of Court Interpreters in Scotland*. Unpublished manuscript

West Midlands Probation Service Bulletin, No 2. 1995

See also the series of introductory books mentioned at pp114 and 130

Expanded List of Contents (Chapters 1 to 9)

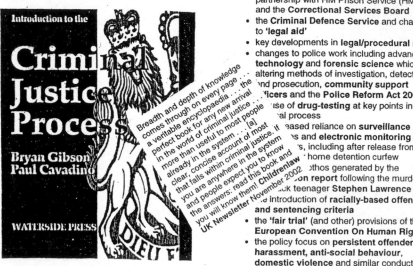